The Elegance of Edwardian Railways

No. 401, the first of Ivatt's Class K1 0-8-0s for the Great Northern Railway, which eventually reached a total of 55 by 1909. In immaculate condition, almost certainly when new in 1901, it is seen near Hadley Wood.

The Elegance of Edwardian Railways

British locomotives portrayed through the camera of James Grimoldby

Geoffrey Williams

OPC

Oxford Publishing Co.

Dedication

This book is dedicated to Mr Grimoldby and his fellow pioneering railway photographers, to whom we owe so much. To Brian George Williams (1947-1989) whose efforts saved this collection for posterity. Finally, to my companion and devoted enthusiastic dog, Horace 'the horror' (1988-1991). A victim of the railway's main rival, the motor car, and yet another driver with his mind not on the job in hand.

A catalogue record for this book is available from the British Library

ISBN 0-86093-477-2

Oxford Publishing Co. is an imprint of Haynes Publishing,
Sparkford, near Yeovil, Somerset, BA22 7JJ

Printed in Great Britain by Butler & Tanner Ltd, Frome and London
Typeset in Times New Roman by Character Graphics, Taunton, Somerset

Publishers note: The illustrations in this book are reproduced from the original
photographic prints of Mr J. Grimoldby, many of which measure only about
70mm x 95mm, and have been reproduced to what is believed to be the optimum size.

Contents

Acknowledgements

It goes without saying, that without the devoted, but no doubt rewarding, efforts of the photographer this book could never have got off the ground. However, as the modern day legions of railway photographers, (who can be found at almost any station in Britain), know, it takes far more than a collection of photographs to make a book.

I am particularly grateful to the OPC railway books editor, Peter Nicholson, along with his staff. Their collective will and desire to produce a high quality book with which to display the contents of this important collection, and not produce yet another 'picture book' deserves the highest praise.

Though not purporting to contain any primary historical material, other than the photographs, the research has been surprisingly lengthy and time consuming. I am deeply indebted to Hampshire County Libraries, whose Railway Collection at Winchester was invaluable, although access to the 'reserve' collection, and staff assistance, could have been improved upon; what are these for if they cannot be used? No such comments could be aimed at the Librarian and his staff at my local branch in Portswood, Southampton. They treated my many requests for books almost as a challenge, gave many alternative suggestions and could not have been more co-operative. Humberside County Libraries also provided useful assistance, as did Peter Nicholson, who turned up trumps when all else failed.

My attempts to give each of the railway company 'mini histories' a bit of life, instead of trotting out the usual facts, owes much to the many hours of historical argument with my former boss and Headmaster, Mr Richard Brent. A true 'great' in his own field, he would no doubt have succeeded equally well had he turned his considerable energies to historical research. Our interpretation of events differed wildly, so do not accept my portrayal of any one railway as 'gospel', merely my own opinion; perhaps acting as a springboard for your own thoughts.

To my late, former university friend, Mr Tim Bennett, who had no interest in railways, fell the task of reading the initial manuscripts. His advice was invariably useful, thoughtful and worth acting upon (quite out of character really), although I did ignore his "burn the lot" parting comment... Tragically, as with my brother and beloved dog, Tim was another fatal victim of Britain's ever growing 'barmy-army' of idiotic drivers, killed while riding home on his bicycle, between finishing the book and its publication.

I must thank Christine and Antoinette for not displaying too much joy at all my enforced absences, and for putting up with all my clutter left around the house. Amstrad, provided an 'idiot proof' word-processor to write this (and my other two books, plug-plug). Finally, I must thank my late dog, Horace 'the horror', for not destroying any of my research notes, after he spent one afternoon happily spreading hundreds of these around the floor of the dining room: "that's the last time you'll be left with a free run of the house, mate".

Well (if you read the 'Dedication' you will understand why) it will be Horace's last time now; with about 5,000 deaths of people, to say nothing of dogs and other wild and domestic animals, each year on Britain's roads, is it not about time we had compulsory, and meaningful, driving tests, of a much higher standard, every six months? Whenever I have raised this with the Department of Transport, or politicians, they take me to be mad. Yet each year we endure all those deaths, tens of thousands of serious injuries, hundreds of thousands of minor injuries and crashes, and millions of 'near misses', all because of bad driving, due to a lamentable standard of driver education, (and no official attempt to even maintain this), and personal idleness. Can governments go on ignoring this slaughter and not encouraging a greater use of our railways? Me mad? I think not.

Geoffrey Williams
Portswood, Hants

Mr James Grimoldby: The Man and His Photographs

It was unfortunate that I met the man responsible for this fascinating collection of historical photographs near the end of his long and eventful life. I was introduced to him by my brother, back in the 1960s, as a young schoolboy with a fledgeling interest in railways. It was, of course, a sad time, when the beloved steam engine was being brusquely pushed aside, in favour of the often unpleasant smelling, noisy and relatively characterless diesel locomotive. The very existence of railways themselves was brought into serious question, in the face of the onslaught of the motor vehicle and mass, personal transport. Yet, at the age of eight, I happily exchanged my extensive, all-metal, 'push along' railway, not for a Scalextric racing car set, but a Hornby Dublo electric railway, much of which was passed-on by my brother.

Following that, and regular travel by train, came the hobby of train spotting, and what I found to be the sheer 'magic' of railway history. It was at this stage in my life that I met this 'larger than life' character, who was well into his eighties. My enthusiasm for history generally, and railways in particular, clearly rolled back the years for him, and over a period of time his many, and varied, mementoes were dusted down and brought out from years of almost forgotten seclusion.

Of course, railways were our main topic, but he had wide-ranging interests and the fascination, and character, that could hold one spell-bound for hours on end. However, his real interest in railways, judging by the publication dates of books he gave me, waned shortly after World War One; replaced by aeroplanes, ships, and (oh dear) motor cars. These in their turn seem to have fallen victim to an interest in war history, while he also had a collection of lead soldiers.

As a youngster, I relished the stories about things he had done, and especially his travelling exploits. It did not occur to me that I ought to be recording specific details about his life and background. He was always Mr Grimoldby to me, and whatever else I knew about him came through his stories, many of which, alas, are now vague memories.

The 'collection', as such, came into my permanent possession on his death, and is mounted in three large notebooks, with brief comments written alongside, in the most elegant of hand writing. Not all the photographs were taken by Mr Grimoldby, and those that were not, apart from being the best documented by far, have been duly accredited, but I have mostly used his own photographs. However, while having to wade through nearly 300 books, countless magazines and other collections for research purposes, I came across a small number of photographs claimed on behalf of other photographers, that are in Mr Grimoldby's 'collection', seemingly taken by him. Alarm bells began to ring.

This situation seems to have arisen due to the, as I understand, close camaraderie among those pioneering railway photographers. Recollecting stories told by Mr Grimoldby, I assumed that he travelled around with a group of photographers, as he spoke regularly about them. In retrospect, it is more likely that, as friends, they exchanged duplicate photographs with one another, bearing in mind that travel, and especially photography, was relatively expensive in those days, and that they met up only occasionally. I was told many stories connected with individual photographs, and Mr Grimoldby's memory was clear enough to remember the names of several engine drivers, which is presumably why so many would 'pose' for the photograph, or even manoeuvre their engine into a suitable position when on the sheds. I was, therefore, quite surprised to find several photographs, dated between 1898 and 1903, published and credited to Ken Nunn, and not just from his 'collection', when he would have been aged about 7-12 years; Mr Grimoldby would have been about 25 years old in 1903.

One of these, now badly faded, shows a GNR Stirling 8ft single racing through Hatfield at 70mph, taken from the lineside, just over one yard from the track. The camera 'eye level' is that of an adult, and not a 10-year old boy; not that such a youngster would surely be allowed to set up his heavy camera in so dangerous a position. In this instance the evidence suggests a mistake has been made regarding the identity of the photographer and, I suspect, there are others.

Mr Grimoldby mounted his 'collection' before World War One. I would suggest, therefore, that a question mark remains as to who took the few pictures in question (there is even one photograph, not re-produced here, claimed elsewhere for another photographer which Mr Grimoldby has accredited as being given to him by someone else). Ownership of any glass-plate, and other, negatives would go some way towards establishing the identity of the photographer, but from what I remember of Mr Grimoldby's, those that have survived are likely to be in a pretty poor condition.

Unlike today, outlets for railway photographs were quite rare in late Victorian/Edwardian England. One common use, was for the pictures to be painted over, to form the basis for sets of post cards. The Locomotive Publishing Co. had a major share in the market to provide the photographs to post card manufacturers, and it obtained pictures from amateur photographers, among other sources. I do not know if Mr Grimoldby sold any pictures to them, but he did take some photographs specifically for at least one railway company, the GNR, while he also had pictures published in books. I particularly remember him pointing some out in W. J. Gordon's *Our Home Railways*, as he then gave me the books in question. There were, presumably, other outlets as well, but Mr Grimoldby was not a professional photographer and such records were not kept, or at least shown to me.

What the above might do is to stir up the odd hornet's nest, especially as some railway photograph collections are now passed off as though all the photographs were taken by the owner. However, as an historian, and all too aware of the lamentable depths railway 'history' displays with its lack of historical perspective and questioning, a shake up in this respect will only be of benefit.

The 'collection', as such, of Mr Grimoldby refers to those three aforementioned books. They, like a great many other books, photographs, post cards and so forth, remained packed away in boxes for years and had been largely forgotten. These, and many other little 'treasures', only gradually came to the surface again after I arrived on the scene. One wonders what would have happened to them had he not met me, as Mr Grimoldby had obviously not bothered with them for decades.

Following his death, in the late 1960s, several boxes were passed on to me which contained books, magazines, glass-plate negatives (mostly damaged or broken), timetables, photographs and post cards. Needless to say, I felt as though all my Christmas's had arrived at once, despite sadness over his death. I still have many of these, though a number of photographs, not mounted in the book 'collection', and glass plates were never returned after being sent for inspection in London. I still retain other items, although some were lost when I loaned them to suitable interested parties (never again).

In many respects, the photographs which form the 'collection', along with the other paraphernalia, could have found a more sympathetic custodian than me. When the time came to leave home, in my late 'teens, the 'collection' was once again packed away into boxes, only emerging on irregular occasions.

The idea to have these published, in a format which I considered worthy of their historical and, in certain cases, artistic value, came when living near York, with my regular visits to the National Railway Museum. I was requested to deposit the 'collection' at the NRM so as to give them a wider audience, and to make them available for historical research. Though I considered this a good idea, I felt that a book would be a much more suitable vehicle for bringing them to the attention of interested people, and would meet with Mr Grimoldby's approval, despite the cost; photographic books are not, alas, cheap to produce. With the emphasis placed on the quality of reproduction, I have been absolutely delighted with the publisher's concern and efforts; not all authors can say that.

Photography at the turn of the century had lost the 'black art' mystique of earlier years, but was far from being a popular hobby. Unlike today, when the swarms of railway enthusiasts bristle with cameras and lenses, they were pretty thin on the ground. You had to be keen to pursue this particular hobby, as quite

apart from often having huge and heavy cameras, taking an age to set up with their glass plates and their many technical drawbacks, you then had to develop and print to get the results; no 'point and press' picture taking and then off to the developers in those days.

Mr Grimoldby had several cameras, which in themselves must have presented a chronological collection from the first half of this century. The most impressive was a large wood and brass affair, which would have contained quite a number of the box 'Brownies' I proudly owned. Its condition was not very impressive by that time, but my recollection is of the sheer weight and bulk of the thing. Had camera technology not improved, I think that photography would have remained a distinct 'minority' hobby. That was used for his railway photographs, but I also remember being shown another large, black camera, quite a bit smaller than the wooden one, which had a lens held in what looked like a long concertina. He also used a small camera not unlike the pre-World War Two box 'Brownie', much to my amusement.

Yet, despite such primitive equipment, railway photography had its advantages, about 1900. A quick glance through this book will reveal how keen railway workers, and others, were to be photographed with an engine. True, this also reflects pride ("This is *my* engine") in one's work-place, but the rarity of a photographer must have gone some way towards the obvious 'positioning' of an engine to be photographed. Quite understandably, few drivers or shed staff would be prepared to manoeuvre an engine, or to 'pose', for a photograph today, or else BR really would grind to a halt.

There was also a strong bond of friendship among those contemporary photographers, as often happens with 'minority' groups. Undoubtedly, pictures were swapped, and one could surmise that other details, such as technical tips and locations, were freely exchanged. Perhaps there was a feeling of a certain 'pioneering spirit' as well; the thought that one could easily be creating a 'first' with a particular photograph. Anyone who has been involved in the formative years of something new, whether it be motor racing, computer technology or pop music, will understand the satisfaction gained from the knowledge that you are one of the first to ever undertake a certain act. Was this the 'golden age' of photography?

It is indeed fortunate for us that those pioneering railway photographers took to their task with such enthusiasm. We can count ourselves very lucky that so many pictures have survived, and can now be reproduced to look like the originals. When I first saw these pictures with Mr Grimoldby, each one seemed to have a story attached to it. While not expecting to recreate the 'magic' of a personal story, I have tried to give the book the flavour of Edwardian railways, and also the world in which they existed. Within these pictures are contained the ancient and modern in railway technology, at the time; fine details for modellers; and many a veiled comment on contemporary Britain. All hidden behind the thin Edwardian 'veneer' of respectability.

Edwardian Railways: A Golden Age?

There has been an ever-growing tendency over the last few years for 'nostalgia' to taint our sense of history; a hankering after the 'good old days'. This can be discerned in the increasing popularity of television programmes, such as *Poirot* or the *House of Eliott*, the rise of the preserved railway that faithfully recreates a particular era, and the growth of the 'working museum', which generally eulogises about 'days gone by'. Lower down the scale is the rise of the historical 'theme-park', which specialise in the sale of 'nostalgia', while the growth in demand for 'collectables', such as Dinky Toys or Hornby Dublo trains, show that there is a more than healthy number of people who try to recreate their formative years; mostly men! 'Nostalgia' is now a powerful force, but as for looking into, and analysing, the past, this is the lowest form of 'history'.

King Edward VII reigned from 1901 to 1910, and he was reputedly as jovial a character as his mother, Queen Victoria, was austere. As such, he fully typified what is today thought of as the gay and lively 'Edwardian era', which it was if you were one of the very lucky, wealthy few. That era has suffered from the 'nostalgic' interpretation of history, but not so much in recent years. Today, thanks to the intervention of World War One in 1914, the 'Edwardian era' is usually thought of as running from 1900 to 1914, and for the purposes of this book, those are the defining years that will be used.

A modest amount of research revealed the Edwardian period to be the 'Golden Age' of soccer, cricket, hats, the motor car, trans-Atlantic liners, gourmet, pubs and even the British economy; all at a time when poverty affected something over 30% of the population. Nostalgia has heightened the need to link years together, give them a title and to look back on those years as an era, with each year being seemingly indistinguishable from the 'era', such as the 'roaring-twenties' or 'swinging-sixties'. Do railways of the Edwardian era justify such an imposing title as the 'Golden Age'?

That is a matter for interpretation. If we take a 'Golden Age' in the literal sense, as the first of the four classic 'ages', gold being the highest before (human) deterioration set in, then the 1820/30s are more suited, being the formative years of railways, before greed and the drive for profits overtook all other considerations. However, if we assume the 'Golden Age' to be the best, or most prosperous period, then we have a case to answer; the Edwardian period often being described as such, on many occasions.

The last years of the Victorian period, through to 1914, saw the British economy recover from the so called 'Great Depression'. Profits soared to new levels and unemployment fell, yet Britain was overtaken economically by the USA, more than equalled by Germany and was being rapidly hauled in by the emerging economies of France, Japan and Russia, if at a distance. Still, with the change of monarch, the British aristocracy, upper and middle classes abandoned their Victorian imposed self-restraint, and began to display their riches in an orgy of self-indulgence never before seen on such a wide scale and, indeed, only barely approached since with the emergence of the Thatcherite legacy of the 1980s; the Yuppie and other members of the acronym set.

Britain had, at that time, the largest empire in history, on 'which the sun never sets'. The myth was purported that throughout the empire Britain was spreading civilisation, education and Christianity to heathen 'natives', supposedly only too grateful for British 'help'. Nowadays, we know only too well that the price paid for this un-asked for 'help' was far out of proportion to any gains, if indeed gains there were. By 1913 Britain's overseas investments totalled £5$\frac{1}{2}$ billion, roughly two and a half times Gross National Product, of which 65% was in the formal, and informal, empire. London stood at the centre of the world's financial stage, and nearly all Empire trade was carried in British ships. That was exploitation on a massive scale.

Yet, although total profits increased over and again from home and overseas investments, profitability, as measured by the profit per pound sterling of capital invested, was falling. British industrial competitiveness abroad was being eroded, replaced by cheaper German and Japanese products; little has changed since. One popular thesis for this phenomenon is that of 'entrepreneurial decline', whereby the capitalist class became more concerned with enjoying the fruits of their investments, rather than making more money. There was more 'empire building' through promoting grandiose, prestige schemes, rather than purely commercial ones. In many respects British railways, or at least the major ones, began to fall into this latter trap, measuring success in terms of scale, rather than the rate of return on capital invested, with ordinary shareholders often being the immediate losers. Some historians, notably C. P. Kindleberger with "Obsolescence and Technical Change" in *Bulletin of the Oxford University Institute of Statistics,* XXIII (1961), suggest that with the close ties to the important coal industry, railways were a classic case of falling profitability leading to economic decline. That this thesis has been heavily debated for three decades, serves to show that it has some credence.

Railway building continued throughout the period from 1900 to 1912, with mileage expanding from 21,855 to 23,441 in the United Kingdom, albeit at a much slower rate than in the halcyon years of 1840-70. Of those new lines, over 1,300 miles were built in England, with the GWR being particularly active. There were few new destinations reached, as most of the lines were built for either route-shortening purposes, as on the GWR, or duplicating routes in the 'empire building' mould.

Furthermore, as the GCR 'London Extension' shows, railway building was becoming more expensive and capital absorbing. The days when housing in towns was swept aside without compensation, to make way for the new railway, were over. Influential rural landowners were still able to extract huge sums for land lost, or insist on costly deviations "so as not to spoil the view", and the very excellence of contemporary civil engineering techniques did not come cheap either. The financial returns from such lines was often marginal, representing a poor use of available capital, and contributed to an overall lowering of profitability for the shareholders and, ultimately, the national economy. Still, there were very few places in Britain not within a reasonable distance of a railway station, and the most advanced transport system available at that time.

The railway companies themselves had diversified into other forms of transport. Docks and shipping were the most popular concerns, and many of the docks around the coast, and European/Irish steamer services, were owned by railway companies. Those services helped to promote further rail traffic onto a company's lines en route to the Continent.

The major competitor to the railways for traffic in the last century had been the canals, and most of those had been bought by the railways. Traffic had, in most cases, been diverted away from the canals, and the inland waterways remained in a very sorry state. This was in sharp contrast to certain European countries, where the two modes of transport existed in harmony, complementing each other. That opportunity was lost in Britain, where competition, far from improving the service, led to the strong getting stronger (the railways) and eventually strangling the weak (the canals). Ultimately, it was the customer who suffered through a non-integrated service; a scenario which was to be repeated to the railways' disadvantage over 50 years later, by road transport. Such lost opportunities to integrate a national transport network, will almost certainly be put completely in the historical shade by the thoroughly 'political' transport policies of the governments of the last decade or so, to say nothing of the regular 'about-turns' of government (road-biased) transport policies since the railways were nationalised in 1948.

Having already seen off road competition once, in the form of the stage coach, road transport again emerged as a threat to the railways' monopoly of inland transport. In many cases railway companies saw, and realised, the potential threat from the new electric tram and omnibus, and adopted an "if you can't beat them, join them" approach, initiating their own road services which dovetailed into, and complemented, the train services. The financial power of the railways, in particular the main ones like the GWR, meant that they could afford a large number of motor vehicles, offering an important market for both the new manufacturers, and ancillary industries such as tyre makers. This, of course, aided the development of what was to become the railways' chief rival.

Though the railway industry was one of the great monoliths of the economy, it also proved to be quite innovative. Of course, steam power was being continually developed, and what was new and exciting in 1900, such as Ivatt's small Atlantics on the GNR, was decidedly old-hat ten years later. Major strides forward had been made both in carriage comfort and carrying capacity, but these were essentially developments of established techniques. Perhaps of more significance during the Edwardian era, was the use of electric lighting, gas cooking and electric propulsion for the trains. None of those were in widespread use, often not until decades later, but they were important applications for what were fledgeling power industries. The benefits of those pioneering efforts were to be felt throughout society, not always to the railways' advantage.

It would be true to say that, during the Edwardian era, railways played a major role in Britain's everyday life, just like the motor vehicle does today. Even if you never travelled by train, you could bet your last shilling that the food you ate, the clothes you wore, the house you lived in and so on, had been transported by train, or at least the necessary raw materials had. Time itself was 'railway time', and many aspects of society revolved around the railways. For the vast majority of people, any form of lengthy journey had to be taken by train, and it was mainly due to the railways' efficiency that most people could afford to travel at all. Whole towns, mainly on the coast, grew up thanks to the railway 'excursions', as did the public schools. Like today, when our air is heavily polluted by the exhaust fumes from motor vehicles, so the air was polluted by the soot emitted by steam engines. Railways were indispensable; in 1910 railways moved 16 tons of goods per person per year and, on average, each person made $35\frac{1}{2}$ journeys annually.

Perhaps of most importance, in respect of the 'empire building' mentality, was that railways had gradually become an accepted part of the industrial and political establishment. Their economic importance goes without question, but their political clout was considerable as well. Today a great many MPs, particularly Tory, hold directorships and consultancies, from which it is claimed the organisation in question does not gain from their political activities. Likewise, during the Edwardian years a great many MPs were in close contact with, if not in the pockets of, one or more railway companies. This position changed somewhat with the Liberal governments after 1906, and the election of many Labour representatives, but the 'railway lobby' remained a powerful group, to be ignored at a government's peril.

So far I have referred to 'railways' as a block term, but with well over 100 separate railway companies operating in Edwardian Britain, there was a world of difference, in almost every respect, between the giant LNWR and the tiny Lynton & Barnstaple, for example. Each company had its own way of conducting business, often based on out-doing a rival, even if their trains were supposed to connect. The Parliamentary Enquiry into railways in 1917, described them as a "riot of individuality", and cited one company with 41 different types of handbrake on its wagons!

These railways can be grouped by using a variety of measurements such as route mileage, capital employed, dividends and so on. The 'First Division' railways, comprising the LNWR, GWR, MR and NER, were some of the largest companies in the land; indeed, the LNWR had been the largest public joint-stock company in the world at one time. The 'Second Division' consisted of those such as the GNR, CR, LSWR and the LYR, although in terms of mileage the latter railway was out of its depth. The 'Third Division' consisted of the SECR, LBSCR, GSWR and so on; and the GNSR and others formed the 'Fourth Division'. However, even the minnows could be significantly important within their own locality.

There tended to be considerable rivalry and competition between railway companies, much of which was beneficial to the customer. Main line expresses were often fast, frequent and comfortable, as rivals vied with each other to provide the most prestigious services. These improvements were on-going, and progress was particularly rapid during the Edwardian era. Lesser passenger and goods services benefited in the same way, although this was by no means universal. On the other hand, as is often the case with unchecked competition, there was a terrific amount of wastage, particularly with duplicate lines, stations and services.

Such rivalry often permeated down to the lowest grades of staff, and even to the passengers. Railways, though highly capitalised, were very labour intensive, and pride in one's job was undoubtedly more common then, than it is today, if not absolutely so; that may have had something to do with the lengthy hours worked.

There was a certain social esteem attached to working for a railway, as they formed a 'high profile' industry, and were noted as 'good' employers; society was far more concerned with the social hierarchy then, than in more recent years. A railway job was often regarded as a 'safe' job, in a world notorious for an employer's indiscriminate abuse of power; however, it was not necessarily highly paid work. Engine drivers were towards the top of the manual 'pay league', but in 1911, $49\frac{5}{8}$% of railway employees earned less than 25 shillings a week; the respective figures for the cotton and iron and steel industries were $40\frac{1}{2}$% and

$31\frac{1}{2}$%; the average wage being about £1 per week.

In other respects, regarding employees, some railway companies displayed a foresight of the path 20th century industry would take. The NER, in particular, adopted certain management innovations far ahead of those used in most other British industries. Their financial results clearly show the benefits to be gained. Other railway companies, remembering that most people in Edwardian Britain received only minimal, elementary education, embarked on training and education programmes for all grades of employees. Those efforts, though mostly small-scale, were praiseworthy and added to the 'caring' image, while fostering pride and loyalty among employees. Many pictures in this collection show railway workers only too willing to pose alongside an engine for the camera; a sure sign that they were proud of their company and work. Just look at the condition of those engines; even the smallest tank and oldest goods engines gleam like the mightiest express locomotives. Pride clearly manifested itself in a very practical way.

As has been suggested, Edwardian railways seem to have enjoyed a period of unparalleled prosperity and esteem. However, by 1900 there was the occasional dark cloud appearing on the horizon, and 14 years later these had thickened and were closing rapidly. While individual railways were busy competing against each other, thus diluting their resources, new forms of transport were already beginning to challenge their supremacy.

This new competition increased in intensity throughout the Edwardian era and, assisted by the aforementioned 'empire building' mentality, caused a fall in profitability. The following table shows this to good effect:

Year	Total UK Mileage	Capital Raised £m	Gross Revenue	Capital per Mile	Return on Capital Gross	Net
1870	15,537	529.9	£45.1m	£34,000	9.27%	4.55%
1890	20,073	897.5	£79.9m	£45,000	8.67%	3.86%
1900	21,855	1176	£104.8m	£53,500	8.93%	3.38%
1910	23,287	1318.5	£123.9m	£56,300	9.95%	3.6%
1912	23,441	1335	£128.6m	£57,000		

Monetary values alter, as we have found out all too well over the last decade or so, but from 1870 until 1900 prices, and therefore costs, were falling; both began to rise again thereafter, but did not reach the level attained in 1870. That shows the railways did very well in terms of revenue, but just look at the increasing capital cost per route mile! This was the true cost of the blinkered approach taken by many railway directors and managers; Kindleberger has a point.

To counter the fall in profitability, although actual profits might well have risen, some railway companies improved joint working arrangements, thus complementing services. There was also a rash of amalgamations and takeovers, and an attempt by the

GNR/GER/GCR to join together and form a single company was thwarted by the government as being anti-competitive. Experiments were made into alternative fuel sources to coal, which were aimed at improving the coal/water/oil consumption of the modern locomotives, to reduce costs. Some success with the varied cost reducing ideas was achieved, as between 1900 and 1910 the capital cost per mile increased at less than average price increases, and the net return on capital showed a modest rise.

There was, however, still far too much competition between railways for their own good. Even before 1900, many companies had been losing commuter traffic, particularly to the horse-drawn and electric tram. The case of the NLR, which never really recovered, was perhaps the best known example of the effects of such competition. A little later came the horse-drawn omnibus, and early this century the real threat, the motor bus. Almost at a stroke, railway services were hit by this rival that could, in certain cases, pick you up from outside your house and deposit you in the High Street, or at your place of work. Furthermore, buses were often cheaper, had padded seats, and cut the very latest dash in modern travel, unlike the smelly, old steam trains. Okay, so they broke down occasionally, but that was surely a small price to pay for progress.

It is very easy to under-rate the effects of the tram and motor bus competition. By 1914 there was over 2,500 miles of electric tramway in Britain, apart from the horse-drawn tram routes, and by 1910 over 1,000 motor buses were operating in London alone; this in the first years of the petrol engined vehicle. If the railway companies were oblivious to this new competition in 1900, they were more than wide awake to it on the eve of World War One.

The formative decade of the motor vehicle as a practical mode of transport, beginning in 1905, saw very rapid strides forward being made. Initially, the motor car was not a serious challenger to the railways. They were restricted by poor roads, unreliability, speed limits, problems with getting fuel and spares and, most importantly, cost. A decent sized car in 1905, with a closed saloon body for the passengers, say a Napier or Renault, would cost about the same as, if not more than, a private aeroplane does today; in other words motoring was only for the extremely wealthy. Ten years later, on the eve of World War One, there were well over 100,000 private cars running in Britain, and nowhere near that many extremely wealthy people. The writing on the wall was growing ever larger.

It did not take motor vehicle manufacturers long to realise that there was another lucrative market to attack; commercial transport. In those days motor vehicles were built as a motorised chassis, and the body, for people or goods, was fitted on afterwards; tailor the body to suit the purpose. In any case, bodies were often fitted to the chassis by a separate coach builder. As with the passenger motor vehicles, the commercial vehicle was mainly used for local journeys and, as such, did not pose too much of a threat to the railways before 1914. Indeed, in many parts of Britain the local railway owned most of the vehicles, and privately owned ones were used to improve deliveries via the railway. However, the potential for competition from this source was being established.

Road transport in general, steadily becoming the main threat to the railways' monopoly on inland transport, was still dominated by the horse, even in 1914. Most of the examples cited as a threat to the railways were variations of the railways' theme; a transport service. Even personal transport, again restricted to those wealthy enough to afford such luxuries, still included the horse-drawn carriage, not suitable for anything other than short journeys. The advent of the motor bike, or more correctly the motorised bicycle, spread the personal transport option a little further down the social scale, especially for those enthusiastically inclined. It was, however, the pedal bicycle, effectively dating from the 1880s, which had the most effect in this respect.

This little, pollution free mode of transport, apparently making yet another 'comeback' today has, among other things, been credited with being responsible for giving women more personal freedom and changing styles of dress. The female cyclist could not be a 'pretty little thing', ready to 'swoon' into the arms of a dashing man if she expected to be able to cycle into the teeth of a gale. Undoubtedly though, the bicycle was the first form of mass, well popular, personal transport and, as such, was an alternative to the train. Once again though, it was mainly used for short journeys, or in conjunction with the railway on a longer journey. The point to be made is, that the challenge to the railway transport monopoly was rising on several different fronts throughout the Edwardian period, and it was a challenge that, in the main, the railways failed to meet. By 1914 there were over 400,000 of all types of motor vehicle on the roads of Britain; about one for every 100 people.

With regard to the railways' dominance of inland transport, far from being the 'Golden Age' of railways, the Edwardian era might be described as the 'swan-song' of railways. Only a decade after 1914 another form of transport was to challenge the railways, the aeroplane, although, like the early motor cars, that too was also only for the wealthy. Car, bus, motor bike and lorry gradually nibbled away at the railways' patronage, enticing this away with better flexibility, and often lower cost. The railways fought back, but it was only during the last decade or so that the drift away has been reversed, and this is restricted to passengers. Does the government really believe that a fragmented, privatised system will continue that trend? This has been despite a continued improvement in train services, resulting in the Regional Railways and InterCity services of today. The speed, intensity and cost of these, on lines that remain open, would have made the

Edwardian rail traveller stand back in amazement, if not on grounds of cleanliness and ambience; the price of railway cost-effectiveness has been very dear.

Was there anything the railways of Britain could have done to alleviate their relative and overall decline? In the long term, probably not, although there was no need, or sense, for successive governments to forcibly contract the railway system to its present size. There was, and is, something inevitable about the rise of the motor car, from the novelty, through the status symbol to the so-called essential. There is now more than one motor vehicle for every two people in Britain; like the railways before, it has a dominating position in our lives. As has been suggested, however, the management and directors of many railway companies did not help matters during the Edwardian era, with their almost anti-commercial, 'empire building' approach to what most definitely was a business.

Over the years many people made vast fortunes out of the railways, and a great many more achieved above average returns on more modest investments. Many an author, such as Agatha Christie, or 'lounge lizards' in the Bloomsbury set, owed their beginnings, or indeed whole leisured life, to the family's railway 'investments'. If Britain had a nationalised railway, like Belgium and certain other countries, from the earliest days, with anything other than the ridiculous ad hoc attitude of successive governments towards a national transport policy, then perhaps the railways would have fared better. Certainly, ploughing profits back into the railways and adopting a more business-like public service approach to the running of them, would have

helped preserve the formerly exalted position they held in society. Change was inevitable, given the competition, but did the position of Britain's railways have to fall so low?

Looking within the operation of the railways, I would suggest that a very blinkered view was being taken by those who ran them during the Edwardian era. Mindless decisions were taken, based on esteem rather than commercial logic. The GCR 'London Extension' is the classic example of this, but how many other railways failed to pay a dividend? Yet, and there is little doubt about this, the Edwardian period is one of the 'great' eras of both train running and services. Many aspects of rail travel reached their zenith at that time, particularly the care and cleanliness afforded to trains and stations. This was a lumbering, rather than a dynamic, efficiency though; a way of life rather than a service for life; complacent.

Despite everything, Edwardian railways, as with the contemporary economy, gives the impression of being a 'Golden Age' for the industry. Likewise with the economy, this was an age of a squandered opportunity to establish the railways as a true network; a veneer of gaiety, often bolstered by growing profits, hiding absurd inefficiencies. Opportunities have been missed on several occasions since then, and still governments run the railways as a business rather than as an economic and social asset. It is all too easy to look back and point out wrong decisions and mistakes. In this case, it is our error to have judged the Edwardian era too leniently. Perhaps this 'Introduction' ought to have been entitled "Edwardian Railways: A Lost Golden Opportunity?"

Great Northern Railway

In 1900 the GNR main line, running north from King's Cross, boasted the fastest express service in the country; little has changed since. This is probably one reason for its continued popularity with railway photographers down the years. In this collection of photographs, the GNR has more than twice the number of pictures than any other pre-grouping company. Hence, the major problem has been one of what to exclude. In keeping with the character of the railway, I have tried to include as many 'action' pictures as possible.

The Act of Parliament which authorised the building of the London to York direct line was passed at the height of the 'railway mania', in 1846. William Cubitt was responsible for the engineering of this new route, and he took advantage of the experience gained through two decades of railway building elsewhere, to build a route relatively free from long, steep hills and onerous curves. The resulting line was most suited to high speed, and has needed relatively little alteration over subsequent years to keep it right at the forefront as Britain's premier railway 'race-track'.

The section from London to Peterborough was opened in 1850, followed by the direct route on to Doncaster, via Grantham, in 1852. The new London terminus, at King's Cross, was opened in the autumn of that same year. York was destined never to be reached by GNR metals, and trains from the south arrived there via the Knottingley route of the Lancashire & Yorkshire Railway, until 1870, and on the North Eastern Railway line via Selby, thereafter.

This route was to form the trunk of the GNR system, but by a combination of its own lines, amalgamations, joint ownership lines and running powers, the GNR spread its tentacles to reach Stafford, Cheshire, Cromer, Grimsby, Great Yarmouth and Ripon. Hence, from the 1850s, the GNR was running expresses to Scotland, Manchester, the Lincolnshire coast, the West Riding of Yorkshire and, later, Cromer.

This tradition of fast express trains, along with the almost unbroken rule that each train would only have one engine, necessitated the building of a stock of locomotives well to the forefront of contemporary development at any given time. From 1850 until 1922 the GNR was fortunate in having four locomotive engineers capable of breaking new ground and building express engines that were second to none.

Archibald Sturrock was appointed as Locomotive Superintendent in 1850, having virtually run the Swindon Works of the GWR. He knew the value of a central works, and in 1854 the Doncaster workshops were opened; the previous ones at Boston being both inadequate in size, and off the beaten track once the 'direct' line to the North, had been opened. Initially,

the new works were only used to repair and overhaul locomotives, Sturrock's own designs being built by outside contractors.

In the 16 years before his premature retirement, Sturrock provided the GNR with a fine stud of passenger and freight locomotives fully capable of handling the work expected of them. His mechanisation of Doncaster Works also earned him an inclusion in Karl Marx *Capital* Vol. 1, as an example of workers' skills being replaced by machines, to reduce the cost of labour; (do not believe all the rubbish written about the erosion of workers' skills in the name of 'economy' being a modern concern, it is as old as the hills). Unfortunately, there is only one photograph of a Sturrock engine in the collection, and that has been heavily rebuilt, by Stirling.

Patrick Stirling succeeded Sturrock, having previously been the Locomotive Superintendent on the Glasgow & South Western Railway. He hailed from a family steeped in an engineering background, and his work dominated his life. Stirling's imposing stature befitted his autocratic personality and he commanded the respect of all who worked with, and under, him. Unlike many autocrats though, Stirling did not rule by fear, and the loyalty of his men was amply displayed when thousands stood for hours in the pouring November rain, at his funeral in 1895.

Stirling has been remembered most for his 'single driver' locomotives, in particular the gracefully powerful '8-footers'. These elegant machines were at the head of most important East Coast expresses for 30 years and more, and set standards of running that few other companies could even realistically aim towards. To the late Victorian public, an express train, the fastest form of transport remember, was composed of teak coloured coaches, majestically hauled by one of these green thoroughbreds, its great wheels driving it along with an imperious, distinguished ease. Little wonder that the GNR main line was the most photographed in the country, then as now.

Alongside the 'singles', Stirling's other achievements were more modest. He designed useful 2-4-0 and 0-4-2 mixed traffic locomotives, and a good, if varied, stock of tank engines for the growing London suburban traffic. The 2-4-0s have been compared unfavourably with Webb's "Jumbos" on the LNWR, although this general opinion is based on scant evidence, and the GNR engines were not the backbone of the express service, unlike the "Jumbos".

Perhaps Stirling's ultimate achievement was to initiate engine building, and to expand the works, at Doncaster. Without the establishment of this base, it is unlikely that any of his successors could have maintained and developed the high standards of locomotive design and building, first established by Stirling himself.

Henry Alfred Ivatt was appointed to succeed Stirling and took up the position in 1896. He had been trained at the LNWR works at Crewe before moving to the Great Southern & Western Railway in Ireland, becoming the Locomotive Engineer there in 1886.

Despite the reputation of the GNR for its passenger trains, all was not well with the locomotive stock. Decreasing journey times and the increasing weight of trains, through the use of bogie coaches, meant that the 'single drivers' were not always masters of the job in hand; as one of the illustrations shows, double-heading was no longer unknown on the heaviest expresses. The GNR public image of running the fastest trains was in danger of becoming somewhat tarnished.

More important perhaps, was the shortage of locomotives. In his last few years, Stirling had not fully responded to the director's call for more power from the engines. He steadfastly maintained that his 'singles' were capable of undertaking all express duties. For their part, the directors had consistently refused to sanction the numbers of locomotives Stirling had wanted to build, based on the requirements of the running sheds.

Ivatt was able to get permission to build more engines, and within three years had designed the first British 4-4-2 Atlantic locomotive. This was indeed a notable achievement and soon put the GNR back at the forefront of locomotive development. Four years later though, Ivatt brought out his large-boilered Atlantic, which caused a sensation in the 'optimism' of the early Edwardian era. This relatively huge, green engine seemed to symbolise Britain's assumed dominance of the world. Regrettably for the GNR, as with such misplaced 'optimism' in society in general, these engines never quite lived up to their initial promise, until they were superheated and modified by Ivatt's successor.

Apart from his express passenger engines, Ivatt undertook a rationalisation of the locomotive stock and produced many fine designs of mixed traffic, freight and tank engines. Repair facilities were also much improved and on his retirement, in 1911, Nigel Gresley, his successor, was left with an impressive stud of locomotives, and associated repair and maintenance facilities second to none.

The pictures selected to represent the GNR follow very much the photographer's bias, as with many others of the same period, towards express trains. Excellent though the pictures are, most of the engines will be familiar to railway enthusiasts, but do not let that detract from the sight of Victorian/Edwardian railways at their very best.

This dramatic and brilliant photograph portrays the 10am ex-King's Cross, "Scotch Express", hauled by No. 1007, one of the last of P. Stirling's 8ft singles, built in 1894–5 for the Great Northern Railway. These had enlarged dimensions to earlier examples with $19\frac{1}{2}$in x 28in cylinders, 20 sq ft grate, 8ft driving wheels, 170psi boiler pressure, 16,100lbs T.E. and weighed 45 tons, with just $19\frac{1}{4}$ tons for adhesion. A magnificent sight though the train makes, it comprises a rather mixed bag of coaches for such an important express, even for late Victorian days, with plenty of six-wheelers in evidence. This is railway photography at its very best.

Another of the last batch of Stirling's famed 8ft singles, No. 1008, dashes along near Hadley Wood with an express for the north. The driver appears to be looking towards the camera, but the platelayers take a blasé attitude to this stirring sight, so completely GNR in all respects.

Stirling single No. 1007 is seen in somewhat less dramatic weather conditions than before, as it runs through Harringay. The dress of the two ladies suggests that it was still a bit nippy, or is it a display of Victorian modesty? These last examples of Stirling's masterpiece had an enlarged firebox, but an unchanged boiler, which led to excessive wear in the larger cylinders. These had to be replaced on all the last engines at an early date.

Despite being numbered No. 2, this was the fourth '8-footer' to be built, in 1871. These earlier engines had 18in x 28in cylinders, 140 (later 160) psi boiler pressure, a 15.8 (later 17.7) sq ft grate, and weighed 38½ tons. They originally had attractive open splashers, closed off in this picture, but only had brakes on the tender. Driver Haigh, whom the photographer came to know well, is in the cab of his regular engine, in its latter years. At that time, prior to World War One, Mr Haigh often took excursion trains from Leicester to Cleethorpes, composed of up to 18 six-wheelers, "took a fancy" to the resort and decided to retire there.

Right: No. 7, built in 1873, stands at its home shed of New England. This engine hauled the East Coast trains from King's Cross to Grantham on two occasions during the 1888 'races' to Edinburgh. It managed a best time of 115 minutes for the 105 miles, an average speed of 55mph, as opposed to the 105mph of the fastest train today, and 101 minutes (62.7mph) for the fastest in the 1895 'races' also by an '8-footer'.

Below right: The second part of the 2.30pm ex-King's Cross express dashes through Potters Bar, behind '8-footer' No. 53, built in 1875 in a somewhat faded photograph. These engines, which epitomise Victorian engineering and aesthetic standards, began that rare combination of grace with power, synonymous with the GNR main line, through Ivatt Atlantics to Gresley's Pacifics and V2s and ultimately to the 'Deltics' of the diesel era. Originally designed to haul 150-ton trains at 50mph, these handsome engines were only displaced off the front-line express duties as train weights and speeds increased at the turn of the century. Once away from such duties, the great single driving wheel, and low adhesion factor, made them unsuitable for most alternative duties. They had a few years trundling around the flat lands of Lincolnshire, but withdrawal soon followed, and was effectively completed by World War One, a mercifully short end for such grand thoroughbreds.

Above: Stirling '8-foot' single No. 95, built in 1880, is described as passing Hornsey at 'high speed' by the photographer, with the 10.10am ex-Sheffield, due into King's Cross at 1.30pm. Stationed at Grantham, this engine made five runs in the 1888 'races' over the 82.7 miles between Grantham and York, completing two runs in 89 minutes, the second fastest of the 'races', at 58.3mph net, 55.7mph actual. In the 1895 'races', this was improved to 65.3mph, by a 2-2-2 single. It is seen here in somewhat less graceful condition, as rebuilt by H. A. Ivatt with a domed boiler and a 23¼ sq ft grate.

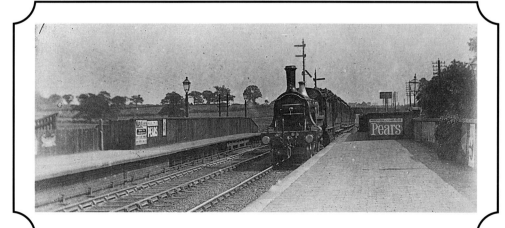

Top: Such a photograph might have been almost the norm on the MR and not uncommon on the LNWR, but was not to be undertaken lightly on the GNR. Double-heading might have been looked down on by GNR employees, but 234 class No. 230, built in 1887 and subsequently modified for pilot duties, and '8-footer' No. 1006 (involved in the St Neots broken rail accident in 1895), make a sight to stir the blood, as they haul the "Scotch Express" through Hadley Wood. These 2-2-2 singles had 7ft 7in driving wheels, 18½in x 26in cylinders, 18.4 sq ft grate, 160psi boiler pressure, 14,220lbs T.E., weighed 39¾ tons and worked in the same links as the '8-footers'. Stirling thought they were actually faster engines than his masterpieces.

Middle: The driver leans from the cab of Stirling 2-2-2 No. 21, the tenth engine to be built at Doncaster works, in 1868, as it heads north through Harringay with an express. These engines were similar to a design Stirling built while at the GSWR, and had 17in x 24in cylinders, 16½ sq ft grate and 130psi boiler pressure. As seen here, rebuilt by Ivatt with a domed boiler, these engines out-lasted many '8-footers' on main line duties, by working Leeds/Bradford expresses in direct competition with Johnson's 'Spinners' on the MR. All were withdrawn by 1913.

Bottom: Stirling 2-2-2, 7ft 7in single No. 874, built in 1892, passes the yards at Hornsey with the 3.48pm King's Cross, on the same day that the photograph of No. 1366 page 25 was taken. This picture offers a fine view of a major railway location at the end of the 19th century, a far cry from today.

At a time when train loads were getting to be too heavy for Stirling's singles, H. A. Ivatt designed twelve modern 4-2-2s, built between 1898 and 1901. The majority had 19in x 26in cylinders, 7ft 7in driving wheels, 175psi boiler pressure, 23 sq ft grate, 14,000lbs T.E. and weighed 47$\frac{1}{2}$ tons. Here No. 383 is seen hauling an 'up' dining car express south of Peterborough, at a fair rate of knots.

Ivatt single No. 261, built in 1900, rests at Lincoln, with the cathedral in the background. This class was the last single driver to be built in Britain and was, until the advent of the 'large' Atlantics, considered to be the fastest of GNR engines. The last one was scrapped in 1918. It is worthy of comparison with the previously illustrated Stirling '8-footer'.

Below right: Ivatt single No. 100, built in 1900, approaches Wood Green with the inaugural run of the 6.10pm King's Cross–Manchester Central express on the 1st July 1905. This was permitted just four hours for the journey, with the first stop being at Sheffield, for which the train was allowed no more than 170 minutes for the 161$\frac{3}{4}$ miles. This exacting schedule matched the fastest time of the lightweight GCR afternoon express to Sheffield, albeit over a shorter route, and was probably the finest example of Ivatt 'single' working to be found on a daily basis.

The driver of the pioneering British Atlantic, No. 990 Henry Oakley leans from his cab while passing Holloway with an express. Due to this engine being built in 1898, the year of the USA 'gold rush', this class of 22 engines (including one 4-cylinder compound) became known as 'Klondykes'. With modest dimensions of 18¾in x 24in cylinders, 175psi boiler pressure, 26.8 sq ft grate, 6ft 7½in driving wheels, 15,850lbs T.E. and weighing 58 tons, with 31 tons for adhesion, these engines had a high relative power output.

'Klondyke' No. 985, built 1900, is passing Hornsey at speed, with the 4.20pm express from King's Cross. This was obviously a favourite location for the photographer, as there are several pictures taken from the trackside hereabouts.

Small Ivatt Atlantic No. 950, built 1900, passes the impressive signal gantry at Wood Green, with the 5.30pm express from King's Cross, on the 1st July 1905. Compared with the earlier pictures the coaches are of a more uniform and modern standard. Some of the trucks in the background are from the GCR.

Another picture of Atlantic No. 985, this time thundering through Essendine station with the 1.30pm King's Cross–Leeds express. In the background a Stirling 0-6-0 waits to take the road south, with a goods train. This one-time junction for branch lines to Stamford and Bourne, no longer even has a station.

Following the success of the 'Klondykes', Ivatt designed an Atlantic with a much larger boiler, in 1902. No. 278, built in 1903, makes an exhilarating sight as it passes Holloway and Caledonian Road with a 'down' express. With 18³/₄in x 24in cylinders, 175psi boiler pressure, 31 sq ft grate, 6ft 7¹/₂in driving wheels, 15,850lbs T.E. and weighing 68¹/₂tons 6 cwt, these were powerful engines for the period. However, their best years came after being superheated and modified by Gresley on the LNER.

The pioneer 'large' Atlantic, No. 251, rests at New England shed, Peterborough. Later versions had 20in cylinders, 170psi boiler pressure and 17,340lbs T.E. When first introduced in 1902, its wide firebox caused something of a sensation, and this engine was portrayed with ever-increasing proportions on advertising hoardings, becoming something of a national celebrity.

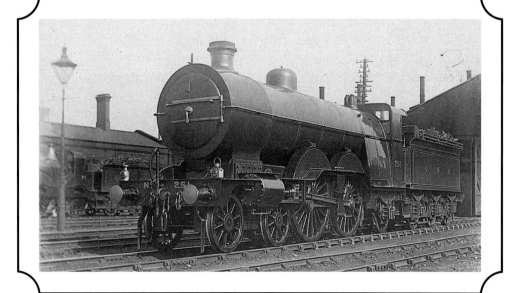

Left: 'Large' Atlantic No. 285, built in 1905, passes Hornsey with the 11.20am Leeds–King's Cross train. Despite being an express, the first three vehicles are vans. These impressive engines, good though they were, performed much better when superheated, first by Ivatt and latterly by Nigel Gresley.

Middle: In 1905 Ivatt built one of his 'large' Atlantics as a 4-cylinder compound. No. 292 is seen passing Hornsey yards with the 4.20pm express from King's Cross, complete with a single indicating shelter on the front. This picture was taken during the 1906 'trials', which included the Vulcan designed compound, No. 1300, and a 'simple' Atlantic, No. 294. The performance of No. 292 was very good, but repair costs were heavy and, as a result, compounding was not pursued. This engine had 13in x 20in H.P. cylinders, 16in x 26in L.P. cylinders and 200psi boiler pressure, which gave 8,995lbs T.E. when working as a full compound. It spent many of its later years working on the Grimsby–Peterborough line.

Left: Stirling 0-4-2 'Greyhound' No. 12, built in 1867, enters Hitchin with the 2.30pm from King's Cross. These free running engines had 17in x 24in cylinders, 140psi boiler pressure, 5ft 7$\frac{1}{2}$in driving wheels and weighed 32$\frac{1}{4}$ tons, with 26 tons for adhesion. These were used for many years on semi-fasts out of London, and also worked on passenger services in the West Riding of Yorkshire. They were equally at home on branch or main line goods trains; little wonder 157 were built. A similar engine can be seen by the shed in the background.

A wonderful picture of Stirling 2-4-0 No. 282, built in 1871, showing the outside frame and slotted splashers. These fine engines had 17in x 24in cylinders, 6ft 7in driving wheels, 140psi boiler pressure and weighed 34¼ tons. They worked the bulk of secondary passenger and goods duties south of Peterborough during the last decades of the 19th century. Reputedly, these engines were not as free running as the GNR 0-4-2s and the LNWR's 2-4-0 "Jumbos".

Stirling 2-4-0 No. 213, built by the Avonside Engine Co. in 1867, with a London bound semi-fast near Potters Bar. Initially used on express trains, these were gradually replaced by the '8-footers', to find their true vocation on secondary duties, on which they could still be seen this century.

It does not bear thinking what Stirling would have had to say about one of his graceful engines being so transformed. No. 708, built by Kitson of Leeds in 1881, wore this inelegant Druitt-Halpin thermal storage system during the period 1905–8. It is seen at New England shed and, whatever the benefits obtained, we must be thankful that this contraption did not catch on in this country.

When he replaced Stirling, Ivatt needed to build locomotives urgently to keep services going, as there was an initial shortage. As a stop gap, he introduced these 2-4-0s; virtually identical to Stirling's designs, but with a larger boiler and grate, and with 17½in x 26in cylinders. No. 1064, one of ten built in 1897, hurries a Cambridge–London express near Potters Bar.

No. 1373, of Ivatt's V3 class 4-4-0, built 1900–2, passes Hadley Wood on a northbound express. These had 17½in x 26in cylinders, 170/175psi boiler pressure, 6ft 7½in driving wheels, 14,382lbs T.E. and weighed 47½ tons. This class was not really intended for GN main line expresses, and they spent most of their lives working from Colwick and Ardsley sheds on Manchester trains.

Another view of a large boilered 4-4-0, No. 1373, running hard through Hornsey with a turn of the century express for the North. In this panoramic railway scene a fireman can be seen, right, giving water to his 0-6-0. This was one of many daily tasks of the steam era so rarely recorded on film, and was unintentionally so on this occasion. No. 1373 survived to be taken into BR ownership.

Despite not being designed as front-line express engines, Ivatt 4-4-0 No. 1389 hauls the "Scotch Express", the premier train of the day. The improvement in coaching stock, in comparison to earlier pictures of this train, is obvious.

Ivatt V3 No. 1366, built in 1900, passes the yards at Hornsey with the 3.45pm express from King's Cross. This photograph was taken only minutes before the picture of No. 874, page 18.

This final picture of an Ivatt 4-4-0 shows No. 1372 crossing the GCR line at Retford South, with the 1.40pm express from King's Cross. This junction was often a hazard to both the GNR and the GCR, yet was not replaced, (by the latter line being tunnelled under the GNR), until 60 years after this photograph was taken.

A fine picture, taken at Hornsey, of Ivatt 0-6-0 No. 332, built in 1896. The crew were proud enough of their goods locomotive to be pictured with it. These engines were similar to Stirling's design of 1892, and had 17½in x 26in cylinders, 175psi boiler pressure, 5ft 7in wheels, 19,105 lbs T.E. and weighed 42 tons 12 cwt.

Another picture of an Ivatt 0-6-0, No. 1105 of the 1897–9 batch, 45 of which were built by Dübs, to meet the locomotive shortage of that period. This engine was the last GNR 0-6-0 to survive, becoming BR No. 64105, and was stationed at Hitchin in its last years. The man in the cab was a companion of the photographer, and appears in several photographs in the collection. This is taken at Manchester and there is a MR locomotive, No. 748, behind.

The driver of No. 192A inspects the tender, right, as it stands in Hornsey yards. This engine was built in 1852 to A. Sturrock's design, by E. B. Wilson & Co., and had 16in x 24in cylinders, 5ft wheels and 140psi boiler pressure. As seen, it has been extensively rebuilt by Stirling, and placed on the duplicate list. Starting life on heavy goods trains, the rebuilding was necessary to enable these engines to continue to perform a suitable role. Such was the original quality of design, that many survived well into this century.

Right: A typical Stirling goods engine, of which 168 were built between 1874 and 1896. No. 847, from one the earlier batches, is near Crouch End on the Highgate/Finchley line, with a typical contemporary goods train. These engines survived many years and had dimensions of 17^1/$_2$in x 26in cylinders, 160psi boiler pressure, 5ft 1in wheels, 17,700lbs T.E. and weighed 36^1/$_2$ tons.

Middle: The crew look from the generous cab of No. 1186, one of the Baldwin (Philadelphia USA) built Moguls. Twenty of these were purchased in 1899/1900 in kit form, and assembled at Ardsley, to meet the locomotive shortage caused by the national strike of the Amalgamated Society of Engineers to protect their status. The GCR and MR also bought engines from the USA at that time. They had 18in x 24in cylinders, 175psi boiler pressure and 5ft 1^1/$_2$in driving wheels, and worked around Leeds and Nottingham on goods and local passenger trains. No. 1186 is seen at Hornsey in 1903, when undergoing trials on King's Cross suburban trains. These were not successful due to the need to turn the engines at the terminus, and also because of their heavy coal consumption. As more engines were built, all 20 of these Moguls were scrapped between 1909 and 1915.

Right: K1 class 0-8-0 No. 423, built in 1901, is leaving Ferme Park with a train of coal empties bound for Peterborough. These excellent engines quickly became popular with crews, and were nicknamed "Long Toms". They had dimensions of 19^3/$_4$in x 26in cylinders, 175psi boiler pressure, 4ft 8in wheels, 28,000 T.E. and weighed 55 tons.

The K1 class was designed to haul 800-ton Nottingham–London coal trains, and also Fletton–London brick trains. They soon proved to be superior to the 0-6-0 engines, being capable of hauling 53 fully laden wagons south, as opposed to 35 by the 0-6-0s, and return north with 60 empties, as against 45 by the smaller engines. "Long Tom" No. 425, built in 1902, is heading south on the main line, with a train of assorted open wagons.

Ivatt's 4-4-2T, of which 60 were built from 1898–1907, was designed for the King's Cross suburban traffic. Though not particularly free running engines, they were quite adequate for the work required, and the majority passed onto BR. No. 1515, built in 1899, is seen near Crouch End with a train bound for Alexandra Palace, mostly made up of six-wheelers, but including one corridor coach.

4-4-2T No. 1502, built in 1899 and which survived to BR ownership, awaits its next duty at Hornsey. These engines had $17\frac{1}{2}$in x 26in cylinders, 170/175psi boiler pressure, 5ft 8in driving wheels, 17,900/18,424lbs T.E. and weighed 62 tons, with 34 tons for adhesion. Condensing pipes were fitted for working through trains to the 'widened lines', at Moorgate. However, their relatively low adhesion weight caused slipping on these trains, and they were soon displaced by the later 0-6-2Ts.

One of Stirling's 0-4-2Ts of 1867, No. 501, rests in between duties at Essendine, after being displaced from King's Cross suburban trains. These had 17in x 24in cylinders, 140psi boiler pressure and 5ft 7in driving wheels, and the 46 engines in the class worked success-fully around London for many years. No. 501 contin-ued to work the Stamford branch, along with some equally vintage coaches; a suitable retirement after many years of hard work.

Stirling's 0-4-2 well tank No. 116, built in 1868 for the London suburban traffic, seen at Hatfield prior to rebuilding, in 1899. The 37 engines in this class had 17$\frac{1}{2}$in x 24in cylinders, 140psi boiler pressure, 14 sq ft grate and 5ft 7in driving wheels. In 1903 this engine was put onto the duplicate list, being renumbered No. 116A. These were very simi-lar to the LCDR "Scotchmen", designed by A. Sturrock, see page 127 for a later version.

At the turn of the century, with the increasing weight, speed and intensity of London's suburban services, more power was needed. Electric traction was becom-ing popular, and the GER tried the 0-10-0T 'Decapod' steam engine. Ivatt's solution was this 0-8-2T, No. 116, built in 1903. It had the 401 class boiler, and long water tanks, with 20in x 26in cylin-ders, 175psi boiler pressure, 17.8 sq ft grate, 4ft 7in dri-ving wheels, 28,000lbs T.E. but at 79 tons, weighed too much. This poor picture shows the locomotive when new.

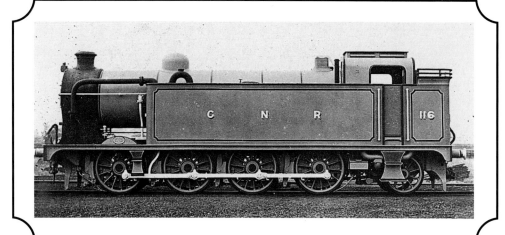

No. 116 was rebuilt in November 1903, with shorter water tanks, an attempt to reduce its weight. It is seen here at Hornsey awaiting its next duty, presumably to Wood Green. Eventually, a further 40 of these locomotives were built, but they were displaced from the London suburban trains by Ivatt's 0-6-2Ts, in 1907/8. Many were sent to Colwick, for short-haul coal trains around Nottinghamshire, a rather sad end for such a purposeful looking class of engine.

These little 0-6-0STs, designed by Stirling in 1867, were very useful engines, particularly for shunting the many coal/brick trains around London. They had 17in x 24in cylinders, 140psi boiler pressure and 5ft wheels. No. 611, built in 1868, is working at Hornsey, complete with half cab and original boiler. Ivatt later rebuilt this with a full cab; far more acceptable to crews.

One of the once-numerous and popular 0-6-0STs designed by Stirling, modified by Ivatt and built from 1892 to 1909. No. 1047, seen here at Hornsey shed, was one of 15 built by Neilson in 1896 to alleviate the GNR locomotive shortage. Like many others of the class, this one passed to BR. These Stirling versions were later rebuilt by Gresley, and had dimensions of 18in x 26in cylinders, 170psi boiler pressure, 4ft 8in wheels, 21,737lbs T.E. and weighed 51 tons 14 cwt. During LNER days, these versatile engines were to be found throughout the southern area.

Another Stirling design, for the London suburban traffic, was this 0-4-4 well tank, of 1872. No. 625 is in excellent condition at Hatfield, when 30 years old. They had 17½in x 24in cylinders, 160psi boiler pressure and 5ft 7in driving wheels. These were popular engines on the outer suburban workings until World War One, despite the increased weight and speeds of the trains, which shows how good the original design was. Some were later transferred to work local trains around Nottingham, thus giving about 50 years service, before withdrawal.

Proudly wearing the headboard 'G.N. Main Line', Stirling 0-4-4T No. 940 is seen with an outer suburban train. These engines, built from 1889 to 1893, were widely regarded as one of the most successful suburban tank engines ever built, drivers much preferring them to Ivatt's later 4-4-2Ts. They had 18in x 26in cylinders, 160psi boiler pressure, 16,800lbs T.E., weighed 53½ tons and were equally at home on the Metropolitan 'widened lines'. Some were later modified with shortened side tanks and an added well tank.

North Eastern Railway

The origins of this company date back beyond the founding of the first railway companies, to the colliery plateways, or wagonways, of North East England. Once the Stockton & Darlington Railway was seen to be a success, small colliery lines opened up throughout the land between the rivers Tees and Tyne. If the Stockton & Darlington Railway had been the catalyst, it was soon to be joined by a number of similar projects; all with the aim of shifting the coals of County Durham to the North Sea ports.

The late 1830s was the period of the first 'railway mania' and York became a focal point for railways in the North East. In 1841 the line between York and Darlington was opened. This was followed in 1844, at the beginning of the second 'mania', by a different company forging north to Newcastle, both lines being engineered by Robert Stephenson.

In 1854 an amalgamation of several of these smaller companies took place, and the NER came into being. Over the next decade or so, several other railway companies were swallowed up, including in 1863, the Stockton & Darlington Railway, the father of them all, and the NER enjoyed a virtual monopoly within its sphere of operation, the aim of all railways. In 1870 the NER finally drove south from York to join up with the GNR north of Doncaster and, with the completion of bridges over the Tyne, at Newcastle, and the Tweed, at Berwick, the direct route from London to Edinburgh was completed.

By 1900, with about 1,700 route miles enshrouding an area bounded by Hull, Doncaster, Leeds and Berwick, and with lines to Tebay and Carlisle, the NER was the largest provincial railway. Although the staple traffic was the haulage of coal and mineral trains to the coast, the NER was one of three companies that owned the London–Edinburgh line. There was enormous prestige attached to the operating of the Anglo-Scottish expresses; this being perhaps even more important than the lucrative revenue derived from such trains. The NER was responsible for providing the motive power from York through to Edinburgh, running over NBR metals north of Berwick. Here was their chance to show what they could do and to impress the Victorian public.

The first Locomotive Superintendent was Edward Fletcher, appointed from 1854 to 1883. He served his apprenticeship with George Stephenson at Killingworth Colliery and assisted in the testing of *Rocket*, prior to the Rainhill Trials in 1829. Fletcher, like many engineers at that time, did not 'standardise'

Soon after arriving as Locomotive Superintendent on the North Eastern Railway in 1885, T. W. Worsdell adopted a system of compounding, initially developed by von Borries of the Prussian State Railways. His first 2-cylinder compound was the F class of 1887, for express passenger duties, of which 27 examples were built. These were very free running engines, and more than capable of carrying out the work expected of them. They had a 18in x 24in H.P. cylinder, 26in x 24in L.P. cylinder, 175psi boiler pressure, 6ft 8in driving wheels and weighed 45^1/$_2$ tons. No. 1542 waits at Leeds Central before taking a Newcastle train. The last engine of this class survived, as a non-compound engine, until 1929.

his designs, and many locomotives were built for a specific task; he would probably not get too far today. Fortunately, one of his 2-4-0 passenger engines, No. 910, has been preserved.

Fletcher was followed by Mr A. McDonnell from the GtSWR in Ireland, who lasted a year in the post. He resigned due to personality clashes; he would probably be more suited to the modern business world! Then came a short period when a 'committee' took over, and the 'Tennant' 2-4-0 design emerged from their deliberations.

In 1885 T. W. Worsdell was appointed Locomotive Superintendent, having held a similar position on the Great Eastern Railway. In five brief years he laid down the foundations for a unified and centralised basis of design and appearance, as typified by the large cabs to protect the crews from the wild easterly winds. He was also a large-scale pioneer in the use of compounding, using two cylinders, and about 250 such locomotives were built. Two of the accompanying illustrations show good examples of his passenger engine designs.

Nepotism in Victorian society was not uncommon,

and one might well suspect a bit of such jiggery-pokery when Wilson Worsdell succeeded his brother, in 1890. W. Worsdell lasted 20 years in the post, and produced many noteworthy designs. He built on the standardisation begun by his brother, but rebuilt the two-cylinder compounds as simple expansion locomotives. By the time of his retirement, in 1910, the NER had a very modern, distinguished stock of locomotives, and a centralised works; whatever the reasons for W. Worsdell initially getting the job, he became one of the most respected Locomotive Superintendents in the country.

It is rather unfortunate that this collection has relatively few pictures of NER locomotives. Some of these are indeed, quite remarkable, but not exactly representative of the stock. There is, for example, no record of the hundreds of coal trains headed by 0-6-0 locomotives en route, daily, to the East Coast ports. Nevertheless, those portrayed show the fine and distinctive lines of NER engines operating in Edwardian England. A fitting reminder of the success of the two Worsdell brothers in transforming the locomotive stock from a mediocre bunch, to that of a highly distinguished pedigree.

A striking picture of Wilson Worsdell's Q class No. 1928, at York. Built at Gateshead in 1896, these were designed for fast/heavy expresses, at a time of rapidly increasing train weights. These had 19$\frac{1}{2}$in x 26in cylinders, 185psi boiler pressure, 19ft 6in grate, 7ft 1in driving wheels and weighed 49$\frac{1}{2}$ tons. They were very sturdy, free running engines, and many lasted well into the 1940s. The comparatively generous NER clerestory-roofed cab is clearly seen here; very welcome in the cold, damp climate of the region.

W. Worsdell's well proportioned S class was introduced in 1899 to eliminate the double heading of expresses between Newcastle and Edinburgh. These caused quite a stir, being the first passenger 4-6-0s in England, but were not really up to the job, due mainly to their relatively small driving wheels for express locomotives of the time. With 20in x 26in cylinders, 200psi boiler pressure, 23 sq ft grate, 6ft 1in driving wheels and weighing 63 tons, they were better suited to mixed traffic, than express passenger, trains. No. 748, of a later batch built in 1907–8, waits between duties at York.

S class No. 741, also from the 1907–8 batch, shows off its lines to good effect, at York. Although looking impressive, as well as lasting until the late 1930s, these were not initially successful when originally introduced in 1899, and a modified version, the S1 class was introduced in 1906. As it happened, 30 more S class engines were built from 1906 to 1919, making 40 in total, for mixed traffic and express goods working, for which they were better suited.

Opposite top: Introduced in 1903, the year after Ivatt's large Atlantic, on the GNR, Worsdell's V class was much more powerful. Built at Gateshead for express passenger duties, these ten engines were highly successful from the outset, and were capable of taking trains of 400 tons, when superheated at a later date. They had 20in x 28in cylinders, 200psi boiler pressure, 23,220lbs T.E., 6ft 10in driving wheels and weighed 73 tons, 39 tons for adhesion. In the 1906 dynamometer car trials, one of these engines ran the 44.1 miles from Darlington to York in 44mins 15secs, pulling 395 tons and reaching 72mph, a good performance for that time, but they were never 'greyhounds' like their GNR counterparts became. No. 1792 was built in 1904, superheated in 1915 and was one of two to survive into BR ownership, just, being withdrawn in March 1948. This view shows the handsome lines to good effect.

W. Worsdell's P1 class, of 1898–1902, enjoyed a long life; many, after rebuilding by V. Raven, were passed onto BR. With 18in x 24in cylinders, 160psi boiler pressure, 4ft 7in wheels, 21,904lbs T.E. and weighing 39½ tons, this class formed the basis of a type synonymous with North East England. No. 2037 shows that even NER goods engines were given a decent cab, being among the best railway companies in Britain, in this respect at that time.

T. W. Worsdell's A class 2-4-2T, was very similar to a design he introduced on the GER in 1884. The NER version had 18in x 24in cylinders, 5ft 7in driving wheels, 160psi boiler pressure and weighed 52 tons. No. 685, built in 1886, is passing Kettleness, on the Whitby–Staithes line. Altogether 60 of these little engines were built between 1886 and 1892. Their usefulness can be gauged by the fact that many worked for over 50 years. In many respects, country stations reflect society's class structure and attitudes to life, at the time of building. 'Bus Stop', unstaffed halts being as representative of the 'pace' of life today, as the grandiose buildings of the Victorian era reflected the more leisured quality of contemporary upper-middle class life.

An interesting, Edwardian view of the central part of Bridlington station. Closer inspection will reveal many aspects of life, as it revolved around the railway at that time. It compares rather favourably with the bland and impersonal atmosphere of the small station today.

Great Eastern Railway

By 1900 the GER moved more commuters into London than any other railway. It also had quite a sizeable traffic in agricultural products, holidaymakers and Continental-bound passengers. With nearly 1,100 of its own route miles and 150 miles jointly owned with other railways, the GER was also one of the larger British railway companies. Thirty years before, however, the GER was financially 'on its knees' and was leading a most precarious existence.

The origins date back to an Act of Parliament, in 1836, for the Eastern Counties Railway to build a line from London to Norwich. At the time, that was the longest line to be sanctioned by Parliament. The section from Devonshire St. Shoreditch to Colchester was opened in 1843, initially with a gauge of 5 feet. The change to standard gauge came a year later following pressure from connecting companies. Through traffic was being contemplated even at that early stage.

A separate company, the Eastern Union, took the line on to Ipswich by 1846, but Norwich was first connected to London, via Cambridge and Brandon, in 1845. Henry Hudson and his fraudulent dealings figured large on the political scene, from 1848, and these seriously under-mined all those companies he was involved with, including the ECR. Nevertheless, a steady expansion of railways took place in East Anglia, with the ECR becoming the dominant company. Eventually, in 1862, the ECR and four smaller companies merged to form the GER, however, there had been too much expansion and not enough consolidation. By 1867 the GER was in a financial mess and it needed a new board, chaired by the Marquess of Salisbury, to put the company on a sound footing.

If the financial basis of the GER was confusing in its

Widely regarded as one of the most handsome steam engines ever built, J. Holden's 'Claud Hamilton' class 4-4-0, No. 1887, built in 1901, climbs Brentwood Bank with the Cromer express; the epitome of Edwardian railways. Eventually, 111 of these engines were built for the Great Eastern Railway, exquisitely turned out in GER dark blue, with most having 19in x 26in cylinders, 180psi boiler pressure, 7ft driving wheels, 17,096lbs T.E. and weighing 51½ tons.

'Claud Hamilton' No. 1860 awaits departure for London, at Cambridge. The elegance of these engines is readily apparent in this picture. This very successful design was built from 1900 to 1911 with little change, except a Belpaire firebox was added to later versions, slightly spoiling the looks. Although rebuilt by J. Hill and N. Gresley, nearly all the 'Clauds' passed on to BR.

early years, so was the locomotive department. There were seven different Locomotive Superintendents in the first 23 years of the company. The comings and goings of the holders of that post resembles the changes of managers at modern football clubs. It seems as though the GER had, in this respect, become a nursery ground for grooming such engineers, until a major company was ready to snatch them away.

The first incumbent of the post was Robert Sinclair, who had arrived at the ECR, from the Caledonian Railway in 1856. He retired in 1866, having designed some useful 2-2-2 locomotives which handled express traffic for 20 years or so.

He was succeeded briefly by W. Kitson and then S. W. Johnson who designed the first English inside cylinder 4-4-0, in 1872. One of his (rebuilt) 2-4-0 designs is shown, depicting several typical 'Johnson' features of his later Midland Railway locomotives, whom he joined in 1873.

Johnson was replaced by William Adams, who came from the North London Railway. He had already designed some useful tank engines, ideal for a busy suburban service, but nothing suitable for long distance work. Within two years of his arrival he designed the successful 61 class 0-4-4T, again for suburban duties. He also designed the first British 2-6-0, for mixed traffic duties. Perhaps his most lasting impression, at least for a few years, was the change of locomotive colour from green to black. Conceivably this was to symbolise the improved financial position of the GER. Like Johnson before him, Adams moved on, in his case to the London & South Western Railway in 1878, and there his designs gained him a reputation as one of the finest engineers of the 19th century. Once again, a loss for the GER.

Adams' successor was Massey Bromley who, although he retired in 1881, was to have quite an impact on the locomotive stock; not least by changing the engine colour from black to the familiar blue. He designed ten 7ft 6in 'singles', 0-6-0 goods engines, several types of tank engine and modified Adams Moguls. This was quite an achievement after only three years in office.

T. W. Worsdell became the new Locomotive Superintendent in 1881. Once again, he added his share of designs to the GER stock. There seemed to be little attempt at either standardisation, or rationalisation; however, his Y14 0-6-0s were still being built in 1913. Worsdell's best known achievement on the GER was the re-introduction, as this had been tried at Stratford in 1850, of two-cylinder compound locomotives. These 4-4-0s were introduced in 1884, but Worsdell left for the North Eastern Railway the following year and the engines were later converted to 'simples'.

The seventh GER Locomotive Superintendent was James Holden, who had worked for the Great Western Railway. He was to remain in the job until 1907 and, during this lengthy period, transformed the GER loco-

S. W. Johnson's No. 1 class, "Little Sharpie", of 1867–71, was designed for light passenger duties, being so successful as to last about 45 years in that role. Eventually, 40 were built, 30 by Sharpe, Stewart in Manchester, having 16in x 22in cylinders, 140psi boiler pressure, 5ft 7in driving wheels, 9,159lbs T.E. and weighing 29¼ tons. W. Adams added Ramsbottom safety valves, closed domes and his own stovepipe chimney, and J. Holden further rebuilt the whole class between 1889 and 1891, moving the dome well forward and increasing the driving wheels to 5ft 8in. No. 34 is at Lowestoft in this latter condition. Fourteen were rebuilt again, in 1900–1, with 160psi boilers. The whole class was scrapped between 1901 and 1913.

T19 class No. 762 is at Stratford, having been rebuilt with a new boiler, cab and Belpaire firebox. The 110 engines of this class were built at Stratford between 1886–97, and had 18in x 24in cylinders, 140psi boiler pressure (180psi as rebuilt), 7ft driving wheels, 18 sq ft grate, 12,530lbs T.E. and weighed 39 tons. Known as "Humpty Dumpties" when rebuilt, they worked main line passenger trains until the 'Claud Hamiltons' arrived. No. 761 was the GER 'royal engine' for many years, while a few, including No. 762, had their tenders fitted with water scoops to facilitate non-stop running from Liverpool St. to Cromer, from 1897. Some were later fitted with a front bogie. They were relegated to secondary duties and scrapping of the unrebuilt versions began in 1908. Sixty were rebuilt as 4-4-0s, and many of these lasted into LNER days.

No. 560, built by Kitson in 1881, rests in the loco yard at Cambridge. Designed by Massey Bromley, the ten engines in this class had 17$\frac{1}{2}$in x 24in cylinders, 5ft 2in wheels and weighed 36 tons 3 cwt. Useful though they were, the class soon became non-standard, and increasing train loads restricted their gainful employment. All ten were scrapped between 1904 and 1906.

Y14 class No. 982, is at Stratford in front of an unrecorded 2-4-0. Designed by T. W. Worsdell, no less than 289 were built between 1883 and 1913, of which 272 became LNER J15 class, and half of these were passed onto BR. Dimensions were modest at 17$\frac{1}{2}$in x 24in cylinders, 160psi boiler pressure, 4ft 10in wheels, 18 sq ft grate, 16,924lbs T.E. and weighing 37 tons, but on the Rev. Awdry's railway the class would have, no doubt, achieved "really useful engine" status.

A typical duty performed by Y14 class engines for over 60 years. No. 890 runs into Ely with a goods train. No. 930 of this class was assembled at Stratford, on 10th December 1891, by 137 people, in 9 hours 47 minutes. All the parts were laid out beforehand, but not fitted, and the engine was finished in workshop grey before being sent on a 30-minute trial. After successfully completing this, it was put on the 560-ton Peterborough–London coal trains for 36,000 miles before going into the shops again, and receiving its coat of black paint. An extraordinary testimony to Stratford's high standard of workmanship.

motive stock from a myriad of designs, none of which were particularly outstanding, to a cohesive stud, usually immaculately turned out. Inevitably, Holden is best remembered for his 'Claud Hamilton' locomotives, as illustrated. These stylish engines formed the back-bone of East Anglian express services for many years, even after the GER itself had vanished. He also designed the first British 0-10-0T Decapod, for use on the London suburban services. Unfortunately, this had to be rebuilt as it damaged the rails.

Holden was also a pioneer in the use of liquid fuel, using waste products from the GER oil-gas plant. About 60 locomotives were eventually converted to burn that fuel, in the 1890s, including members of the 'Claud Hamilton' class. This ended when the supply

from the oil-gas plant proved to be insufficient and the cost of imported oil exceeded that of British coal. Other companies experimented with oil-fired engines based on Holden's principle.

Clearly the GER had been transformed completely from its disjointed beginnings, by the time S. D. Holden replaced his father in 1908. This can be depicted in no better way than through the locomotive stock, and the magnificent new London terminus at Liverpool St., which opened in 1875. With its Continental expresses and steamers, expresses going as far north as York, the world's busiest suburban passenger service and its vast, though seasonal, agricultural traffic and excursion trains, the GER eventually had much for the bigger railway companies to envy.

The crew of F48 class 0-6-0, No. 1190, inspect their steed at Stratford, prior to the next duty. This class was the goods equivalent of the 'Claud Hamiltons', and was similarly successful. With 19in x 26in cylinders, 160psi boiler pressure, 4ft 8in wheels, 24,340lbs T.E. and weighing 44$\frac{1}{2}$ tons, they were very capable engines indeed and complete masters of their work.
Later versions had a Belpaire firebox and larger boilers, and were designated G58 class; eventually the F48s were rebuilt as such.

Adam's 0-4-4T No. 67, of the 61 class, waits at Bethnal Green with a Liverpool St.– Snaresbrook service. The 50 engines in this class were built between 1875 and 1878, by Stephenson, Kitson and, like No. 67, Neilson. Dimensions varied with each builder, but the 1875 Neilson batch had 17in x 24in cylinders, 140psi boiler pressure, 4ft 10in driving wheels and weighed 48$\frac{3}{4}$ tons. They remained successful performers on the intensive Liverpool St. suburban services until well into this century.

With the opening of Liverpool St. station, the need for tank engines suitable for the ever-growing suburban services was of paramount importance. Massey Bromley's solution was the E10 class, of which 60 were built between 1878 and 1883. Similar to the 61 class they had 16½in x 22in cylinders, 140psi boiler pressure, 4ft 10in driving wheels and weighed 44¾ tons. They were capable of accelerating to 20mph within 30 seconds of a start, with a fully loaded train, and the last one was not withdrawn until 1912. The crew of No. 588 have some mouth-watering adverts to contemplate, while awaiting the next turn.

Bromley designed several types of 0-4-4T for passenger duties, those like No. 145, being built by Hawthorn, Leslie and Co. in 1881. They had 16in x 22in cylinders, 140psi boiler pressure, 5ft 4in driving wheels and weighed 41 tons. They proved to be useful machines, and were rebuilt by Holden as 0-4-2s, as seen here, having the boiler pressure raised to 160psi. However, the increasing weight of the Liverpool St. 'jazz' services was too much for these engines, and all were scrapped by 1905.

The 50 2-4-2Ts of Holden's C32 class, built between 1893 and 1902, were the largest with this wheel arrangement on the GER. With dimensions of: 17½in x 24in cylinders, 160psi boiler pressure, 5ft 8in driving wheels, 14,710lbs T.E. and weighing 58½ tons, they were the tank engine equivalent of Holden's 2-4-0 locomotives. No. 1093 is at Stratford, complete with an Edmonton headboard. Once displaced from the Liverpool St. suburban services, many worked on seaside branches, like those at Clacton or Brightlingsea, and the majority survived to serve BR.

North British Railway

By 1901 the NBR was comfortably the largest Scottish railway company. It reached Aberdeen in the North East, via running powers, Mallaig and Fort William on the West Coast, and had routes to Berwick and Carlisle, on the English border, as well as 120 route miles in England. Edinburgh Waverley was the largest station, and the bridge over the Tay estuary the longest, in Great Britain.

The NBR could also claim to be the oldest Scottish railway company, by virtue of it including the Monkland & Kirkintilloch Railway, opened in 1826, amongst those it absorbed; amalgamations played a significant part in NBR history. However, despite the heritage and obvious size of the NBR, it seldom caught the public imagination with its services. Since 1869, the NER ran nearly all the express trains between Edinburgh and Berwick, not exactly reflecting glory on the NBR, while its other main line services, to Aberdeen and Carlisle, were over routes unsuitable for dashing expresses. In this respect, its main rivals, the CR and the GSWR, wiped the floor with the NBR.

With regard to locomotive matters, things could have been better as well. Between its earliest days and the 1923 Grouping, the NBR had nine Locomotive Superintendents, more than any other company bar the GER. Naturally enough, this situation prevented any real consistency of design. Messrs Thornton, Smith and Petrie, served in that position before 1855, followed by Mr Hurst until 1867. Mr T. Wheatley served until 1874, and one of his locomotives is shown. Dugald Drummond arrived from the LBSCR in 1874 and, until he departed for the CR in 1882, did a good job in bringing some form of cohesion to the NBR locomotive stock. Matthew Holmes succeeded Drummond, and progressively built on the foundations laid down by the, later, great man. No. 592 depicted shows the Drummond influence. Holmes was succeeded by W. P. Reid in 1903.

While still short on charisma, the NBR faced the 20th century as a readily identifiable, proud railway, and not a hotchpotch of amalgamations. However, it continued to reflect the Scottish 'work ethic', rather than the perceived glamour of its two main rivals, and was never held in such high public esteem.

Former Edinburgh & Glasgow Railway (amalgamated with the North British Railway in 1865) 2-2-2 6ft 'single', is at Perth. As NBR No. 1003 it was rebuilt as seen, in 1897, and survived into this century, mainly on local passenger duties.

Even the photographer describes this as an 'old' engine, and it certainly looks it. No. 846 was designed by T. Wheatley, and the class was built between 1868 and 1873 at Cowlairs. With 16in x 23in cylinders, 130 psi boiler pressure, 5ft wheels and weighing 36½ tons, these numerous engines were pretty unremarkable performers, even when new. The obvious lack of weather protection would not have endeared them to crews, and they mainly worked local passenger trains.

M. Holmes-designed 4-4-0 No. 592, built in 1886, awaits departure for Edinburgh at Aberdeen, alongside some Caledonian Railway coaches. Twelve of these locomotives were built to work this route, and continued to do so for many years. They had 18in x 26in cylinders, 150psi boiler pressure, 7ft driving wheels, and were a development of Drummond's 'Waverley' class. This engine won a gold meal at the 1886 Edinburgh Exhibition, and looks a credit to the NBR.

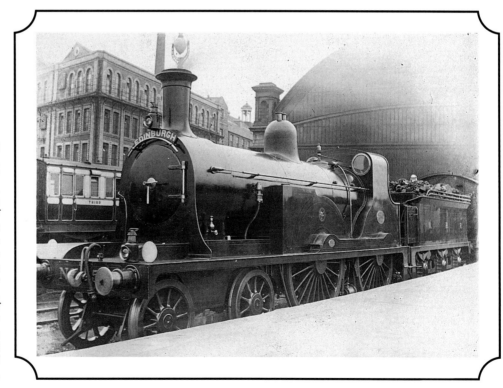

Great North of Scotland Railway

The GNSR was founded in 1845 to build a line from Aberdeen to Inverness. Initial progress proved to be exceptionally slow for those pioneering times, and the line was not completed until 1858. Even then the GNSR only got as far as Keith, where the Highland Railway, building east from Inverness, completed the route; a pretty inauspicious start. Thereafter, several extensions were built, but the GNSR gained a terrible reputation for punctuality (apparently unheard of), disgraceful passenger conditions and an antagonistic attitude to both rival companies, and patrons (who needs the latter anyway?).

Mr Moffatt became General Manager in 1880 and totally transformed the company and its workings. It became possible for passengers to sit in good quality carriages, on trains that ran at convenient times and made connections with other railways (it had not been unknown for GNSR trains to leave Aberdeen station early, seconds before an express from the South arrived, thus missing all connections). Things began to look up for the people of North East Scotland, and not before time.

With regard to the locomotives, the 4-4-0 virtually dominated the scene since the third Locomotive Superintendent, William Cowan, first designed one in 1862. His successor, James Manson 1883-90, designed some 0-6-0T engines, and James Johnson 1890-4, the son of S. W. Johnson of the Midland Railway, some 0-4-4Ts similar to father's, but still the 4-4-0s reigned supreme for both passenger and goods traffic.

By the turn of the century, this small railway company had managed to throw off its poor reputation, and was becoming something of an example as to how an efficient railway should be run, not unlike the LBSCR in England. This was no easy task, and represented a most praiseworthy effort on the behalf of workers, managers and directors; the rewards being an enhanced status both with the travelling public, and within railway circles.

This picture shows the spacious layout of the Great North of Scotland Railway station at Inverurie. Careful examination will reveal many of the items associated with an Edwardian country railway station, the signal above the footbridge being a peculiarity. The engine, although not identified, is a typical GNSR 4-4-0, probably designed by Pickersgill, with 18in x 26in cylinders, 165psi boiler pressure 6ft 1in driving wheels and weighing about 45 tons. Inverurie was the home of the works, and was also a junction.

Great Central Railway

Seldom, in industrial history, can there have been a company quite like the GCR. Beginning life as a localised, provincial concern, as did most railway companies, it went through expansions, amalgamations, take-overs, name changes and diversification into docks and associated activities, until it became one of the ten largest railway companies in Britain.

Early in this century the GCR boasted a peerless express service out of London, with trains formed of possibly the best coaches, and hauled by probably the finest and most handsome passenger engines of the time, all on the newest main line in the country. From being regarded as a 'servant' to the mighty LNWR, GNR and MR, this upstart had brought itself, with undoubted and envied elan, to represent Edwardian optimism in the way its expresses dashed north from Marylebone with a seemingly gay abandon. Yet, it remained an enigma, for not once, since the plebeian sounding Manchester, Sheffield & Lincolnshire Railway changed its name to the GCR in 1897, did it manage to pay shareholders a dividend. Investors had nothing but pride to show for their holdings; (I wonder if those who have invested in the Channel Tunnel will suffer likewise?).

The MSLR was formed in 1847 by an amalgamation of the Sheffield, Ashton under Lyne & Manchester Railway, dating from 1837; the uncompleted Great Grimsby & Sheffield Junction Railway; the Sheffield & Lincoln Railway; and the Great Grimsby Haven Company. At the time of its inception, the MSLR formed one of the largest railways in the country, but the MSLR's role as a supplier of traffic to the LNWR, MR and soon the GNR, was already being established.

The first 30 years of the MSLR's existence was a time of financial stringency. Part of the blame for this was due to much of the traffic generated being passed onto other railways to complete the journey, thus restricting revenue. There were attempts at forming working relationships with other companies, with a view to increasing the MSLR share of the takings from its own clientele, but more often than not these ended in quite fierce disputes. One successful arrangement, with the GNR, was the starting of a through King's Cross – Manchester express, in 1857. Later on, MSLR engines worked down the GNR main lines as far as Grantham, but GNR coaches were used, as MSLR stock was not up to the standards expected by passengers offered a choice of routes.

In 1853 Edward Watkin was appointed as General Manager, becoming Chairman eleven years later; as will be noted elsewhere, he was also the Chairman of the Metropolitan Railway, the SER and the East London Railway, and also a director of the GER and GWR. Clearly, this man had ambitions, one of which

was to form a direct railway link from industrial Lancashire to continental Europe, via a Channel tunnel. It almost goes without saying that Watkin was Chairman of the company formed to build the underwater link.

As might be expected from such a determined character, once Watkin got a grip on the MSLR things started to happen. Throughout the mid-19th century there was a steady expansion of local lines, while new docks were opened at Grimsby, in 1854. Then, in 1866/7, the Cheshire Lines Committee was formed, jointly with the GNR and MR. This was based in Lancashire and Cheshire, and included a Manchester – Liverpool line; the whole system being worked by the MSLR.

Watkin's big plan for the Continental link looked as though it might come to fruition, with the granting of Parliamentary permission for the MSLR to build a line from Annesley, in Nottinghamshire, to the MetR at Quainton, and thence to proceed over the latter's tracks, to a new London terminus. The parallels here with the present Channel Tunnel, and its attendant rail link, are obvious, not in the least regarding the need for a new railway line, other competing modes of transport and the financial viability of the whole project. When the 'London Extension' of the MSLR was being built, in the 1890s, the same considerations were being put forward then, as now, to evaluate the worth of the new venture: a new high speed rail-link, expectations of traffic growth, high construction costs, disruption of peoples' lives and so on. 'Nothing new under the sun', one might think, and is it just coincidence that the new link is to be built nearly a hundred years after the 'London Extension'? This time, the Channel Tunnel *is* a reality, but I doubt that the whole project will be finished before 1999, rail link and all. I wonder if it will ultimately endure the same fate as the MSLR 'London Extension', when it was severed and closed, after only 60 odd years?

Watkin stood down as Chairman of the MSLR in 1894, once permission for the 'London Extension' was granted. The MSLR had never been a wealthy railway, "Money Sunk and Lost", being an unfortunate, but nonetheless accurate, popular nickname in the 1890s. The cost of the new route was phenomenal; rather like the current Channel Tunnel and potential rail-link projects, costs far out-stripped initial budgets, and there was no hope of a state bail-out in Victorian England. By the 1890s, Victorian morality, much vaunted in recent years, had finally acknowledged that people who lost their homes, however grim they might be, would need to be compensated by a railway company; at last a social conscience was beginning to emerge. This did nothing to help the MSLR though and, with other expensive tunnelling and civil engineering schemes, (most essential to the whole project, although some were not), costs spiralled. With the change of name, from MSLR to GCR, the contemporary satirists and music hall comedians, had a field day, at the investors' expense; "Money Sunk and Lost" became "Gone Completely". How right they were.

The final cost of the 'London Extension', excluding that definitely "sunk and lost" in the Channel Tunnel company, was nearly £12 million, 2½ times the annual turnover in 1913. However, at today's prices, that would represent about £2½ billion, for a similar route mileage to the current Channel Tunnel rail link; what will that finally cost?

The new line finally opened to passenger traffic in 1899. Within a few years a relatively large number of light-weight, comfortable, fast trains were leaving the new London terminus at Marylebone, for Leicester and the North. These were the envy of the main competitors, except for the lack of passengers. The new route did not serve anywhere of consequence, without meeting established competition. Man, essentially being a creature of habit, is not likely to change allegiance from one railway to another without good reason, and sadly, for the GCR, this too often proved to be the case. A very useful cross-country route was established though, and links with the GWR grew, with many trains, passenger and goods, passing between the two via the new Banbury – Woodford Halse line.

Engines needed to work the 'London Extension', with its fast, and hopefully heavy, expresses, were rather different to those required on the rest of the system. The early Locomotive Superintendents were R. Peacock, who left in 1854 to form Beyer Peacock & Co., W. G. Craig, 1854–9, Charles Sacre, ex-LCDR, 1859–86 and T. Parker, 1886–93, all of whom designed engines suitable for such a provincial railway; up to the work expected of them. H. Pollitt, who lasted until 1900, built some 4-4-0s and 'singles', with the new line in mind, but though they were useful and attractive engines, they were not expected to haul the fast, heavy expresses hoped for on the 'London Extension'.

J. G. Robinson was appointed to succeed Pollitt, and he designed the kind of engines any contemporary railway company, with ambitions to run fast expresses and fast goods trains, would have been proud of. Steadily, over the last 23 years of the GCR as an independent company, Robinson designed a stud of locomotives to match those of Churchward on the GWR. They were not surpassed for their all round depth until well into Gresley's reign on the LNER, a post initially offered to Robinson. His designs were efficient, economical, handsome and well up to any work asked of them. Quite often, Robinson and his staff at Gorton Works were forcing the boundaries of steam engine design, and they were not content to sit back and copy successful designs from elsewhere, as all too many Locomotive Superintendents seem to have been.

And yet, despite these advances, and the opening of the new Immingham Docks, the taking over of the Wrexham, Mold & Connahs Quay Railway, and the Lancashire, Derbyshire & East Coast Railway, the GCR was, for its shareholders, a commercial disaster. Much of what was built was unnecessary, and with the advent of the motor car only a few years hence, railways themselves were on the defensive; unbridled competition between railways was out. Besides, imagine the public out-cry at a parallel M1 motorway being built, and that would probably be far more use than the 'London Extension' ever was.

A typical CLC five-coach express is passing Northenden, hauled by a hard-working GCR 4-4-0. This route rivalled the LNWR and LYR Liverpool–Manchester lines, and trains were tightly timed to compete. Judging by the piles of sleepers, and the trucks full of ballast, relaying of the track is shortly to take place.

The elegant lines of Great Central Railway No. 194, one of Robinson's first two Atlantics, built in 1903 by Beyer Peacock, are shown to good effect as it is turned at Neasden. This one had 19in x 26in cylinders, 180psi boiler pressure, 6ft 9in driving wheels, 18,000lbs T.E. and weighed 72 tons, with 37 tons for adhesion. A further 25 engines followed suit. These were huge engines for their time, heavier than Ivatt's large Atlantics on the GNR, and the lightweight London Extension expresses presented no problems at all. They lasted well, many passing onto BR.

Gleaming sister engine to that in the previous picture, No. 192, is also seen at Neasden. This was identical to No. 194, except for having 19$\frac{1}{2}$in cylinder bores. This class was quickly nicknamed "Jersey Lilies", after a Manchester pub, and were very popular with both crews and passengers alike. The class dominated the express trains on the Marylebone–Leicester line, until 1936, and often hauled the prestige, pre-WW1 3.15pm Marylebone–Sheffield express, which covered the 165 miles non-stop in 170 minutes, albeit with a lightly loaded train. Speeds in excess of 80mph were commonplace on the falling grades of the GCR main line.

Parker's 2A class 4-4-0 No. 690, built at Gorton in 1894, rests in the then rural setting of Neasden shed. It has been modified with the Robinson chimney and extended smokebox. The earlier members of this class were built by Kitson, and were almost identical to one of their own designs. All 31 engines had 18in x 26in cylinders, 160psi boiler pressure and 6ft 9in driving wheels. They were very useful on secondary duties, and lasted well into LNER days as the D7 class.

The location of Robinson's 1013 class No. 1014 Sir Alexander, *built in 1901, is unrecorded, but the photographer's companion is in the cab. The 40 engines in this class were built to replace the singles on the London Extension and had 18½in x 26in cylinders, 180psi boiler pressure, 6ft 9in driving wheels, 17,730lbs T.E. and weighed 55¾ tons. These proved to be very fast engines with the lightly loaded expresses.*

A marvellous picture of Pollitt's single, No. 969, at Manchester. While not the most elegant of singles, they successfully surmounted the challenge of the 'coupled locomotive', and were not scrapped until 1923–7. Ironically, they did little running on the London Extension, due to the need to bed-in the track, and spent the rest of their days, successfully, on Sheffield–Lincolnshire and CLC services. No. 969 ran for two years with a 180psi boiler, later used on the 'Coronation' tanks. It was also the first locomotive, as seen here, to wear the new standard GCR dark green livery, lined out in black with two white lines.

Pollitt's last design was the 13 class 4-2-2 singles, for working expresses on the new London Extension. With 19$\frac{1}{2}$in x 26in cylinders, 160psi boiler pressure, 24.8 sq ft grate and 7ft 9in driving wheels, these engines were capable of averaging 60mph with the 120 ton expresses. No. 971 is at Neasden with a standard Robinson chimney, and was the only one not to be superheated, at a later date; the only 'singles' so modified. This was the last class of single to be introduced in Great Britain.

In 1902 the first six engines of Robinson's 8 class 4-6-0s were built by Neilson. With 19in x 26in cylinders, 180psi boiler pressure, 5ft 3in driving wheels, 20,000lbs T.E. and weighing 65$\frac{1}{2}$ tons, with 50 tons for adhesion, they were powerful engines, and regarded as being ahead of their time. Finished in a smart black livery, they became known as the "Fish" engines, and spent years hauling southbound fish trains from Grimsby. The driver of No. 1069 has his forward window open for ventilation. In the background some narrow gauge carriages can be seen. This truly magnificent picture has an almost 3D quality about it.

No. 1050, built in 1902, is one of Robinson's 1901 design for an intermediate 0-6-0 goods engine, eventually totalling 174 examples. They had 18$\frac{1}{2}$in x 26in cylinders, 180psi boiler pressure, 5ft 1in wheels, 21,960lbs T.E. and weighed 52 tons. The crew seem more interested in the photographer than in turning their engine, at Neasden depot, a common reaction to the rare sight of a camera in those days.

Parker's 9H class and Pollitt's 786 class 0-6-0s were virtually identical, being built between 1892 and 1902; the last 40 had a Robinson chimney and cab. Having 18½ x 26in cylinders, 160psi boiler pressure, 5ft 1in wheels, 18,781lbs T.E. and weighing 41¼ tons, they were a fairly typical goods engine of the period. Many, including No. 787, built in 1896 by Beyer Peacock, passed into BR ownership.

The 6A class was designed by C. Sacre, for the MSLR, and was built between 1874 and 1880. The crew of No. 351, built in 1874, are clearly proud to pose with their immaculate engine at Manchester despite it being nearly 30 years old. With 17in x 26in cylinders, 130psi boiler pressure and 5ft 3in wheels, these engines were good enough to survive a period of rapid change. The last one was scrapped in 1919, and must have seemed rather quaint alongside a Robinson 2-8-0.

An interesting picture of the interior of Nottingham Victoria station, showing the ornamental brick and ironwork. Parker's 9F class 0-6-2T, built between 1891 and 1900, was widely used around the Midlands on local passenger duties, and had 18in x 26in cylinders, 160psi boiler pressure, 5ft 1in driving wheels, 18,781lbs T.E. and weighed 62⅜ tons. No. 773, built in 1898, cost £2,573 when new, about £500,000 at today's prices, but as it passed onto BR this was well and truly recouped. Immediately behind the engine a small horse-drawn carriage stands on a flat wagon. A precursor of 'Motorail'?

Robinson's 9K class 4-4-2T, built between 1903 and 1905, was similar to engines he designed for the WLWR. With 18in x 26in cylinders, 160psi boiler pressure, 5ft 7in driving wheels, 17,100lbs T.E. and weighing 67 tons, they were intended for the Marylebone suburban services. However, with only 37 tons for adhesion, they were prone to slipping, and were dispersed throughout the system in 1911. No. 1061, built in 1903, went onto the CLC to work Liverpool–Manchester trains, covering the 34 miles in 45 minutes, including one stop. The usefulness of the class as 'stopping passenger' engines is shown by all 52 passing onto BR.

The crew of 5 class 0-6-0ST No. 886, built in 1897, acknowledge the photographer, while shunting at Birkenhead. These useful little dock tanks had 13in x 26in cylinders, 150psi boiler pressure, 3ft 6in wheels, 10,260lbs T.E. and weighed 30⁷/₈ tons. A rather 'cheeky' looking engine, with long chimney, small smokebox door and bell on the cab roof, they resemble the Rev. W. Awdry's Percy.

Hull & Barnsley Railway

Known officially as the Hull, Barnsley & West Riding Junction Railway & Dock Company, it became the HBR in 1905. Launched by certain citizens and the council of Hull, to break the monopoly of the NER and its alleged directing of traffic away from their port, construction began of both the railway and the new Alexandra Dock in 1880. Driven on by local pride, progress was steady, but financial pressures brought all work to a halt four years later. Nevertheless, both railway and docks were opened in 1885.

Unfortunately, the HBR only reached Barnsley through running powers over the MR and, due to the bitter rivalry with the NER, the latter gave it the nickname "Hull and Nowhere Rly". Fierce competition between these two rivals brought down the cost of coal to Hull, and increased its flow. However, the HBR was virtually brought to its knees as the NER had the resources to wage a lengthy commercial war.

Amalgamation with the NER was proposed as early as 1889, and opposed by the Hull council, but a closer working relationship helped to save the fledgeling company. Coal traffic increased steadily, and with a line opening to Wath, in 1902, and running powers being granted into Sheffield, in 1905, even more mines sent their coal via the HBR. Dividends were paid on ordinary shares from 1896, and the HBR future looked increasingly secure.

Passenger traffic was always relatively sparse, even in Hull, where the railway ran on an embankment so as not to cause congestion in the town; another derogatory name used by the NER was the "railway on stilts". Thus, it was the seemingly endless number of coal trains to the docks, that provided those dividends.

Initial locomotives and coaches were designed by W. Kirtley, of the LCDR, but in 1885 Matthew Stirling, son of Patrick Stirling on the GNR, became the Locomotive Superintendent. He held this position until 1922, when the HBR was finally amalgamated with its rival, the NER, a year before Grouping. The engines thus had a unique 'family' look about them, without being stereotyped.

That the HBR not only survived, but performed better with age, had a great deal to do with a more than competent management. Employees were better paid than many of their counterparts elsewhere, and in other respects the railway was benevolent towards them, thoroughly deserving their loyalty. The close relationship between Hull and the HBR was unique in Britain, and worked to the mutual benefit of both, for many years. It was built mainly as a 'coal' railway, prospered as a 'coal' railway, and finally died when the volume of coal shrank in the 1950s, and was concentrated on to the rival NER route into Hull. Without its coal, the HBR line had virtually nothing to support its existence.

The Hull & Barnsley Railway's class 2-4-0s were designed by W. Kirtley of the LCDR, for passenger trains. No. 38, built in 1886 by Beyer Peacock, and rebuilt by M. Stirling with domeless boiler in 1900, is at Springhead shed, in Hull. As rebuilt, the ten engines had 17$\frac{1}{2}$in x 24in cylinders, 150 psi boiler pressure and 6ft driving wheels. Most survived until the 1930s.

No. 33, another of the Kirtley designed J class 2-4-0s, is seen at Springhead shed as partly rebuilt, in 1899. It has received a Stirling boiler, but is otherwise in original condition with 17in x 24in cylinders and 140psi boiler pressure. In 1910 it became No. 33A on the duplicate list, along with the other members of the class.

M. Stirling's first new design for the HBR was the B class 0-6-0 of 1889. These were successful enough to be built until 1908. No. 72 is seen here at Springhead, built in 1898 by the Yorkshire Engine Co. They had 18in x 26in cylinders, 150psi (later, 170psi) boiler pressure, 5ft 1in wheels and weighed 36¾ tons. Though mainly employed on the seemingly endless stream of coal trains running to Hull, they were also at home on local passenger duties, particularly in the Hull area.

Another B class No. 88, built in 1900 by Kitson, is at Springhead shed. This batch had a 170psi boiler pressure and weighed 42¾ tons. In all, 47 engines were built to this design, a considerable proportion of the HBR locomotive stock, and they were withdrawn between 1925 and 1938, after many years of honest toil.

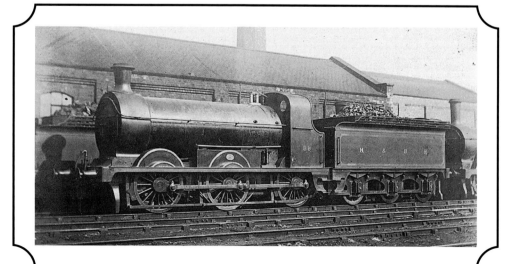

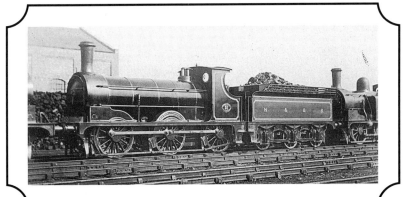

Kirtley's goods engine design for the HBR was soon to be out of its depth as loads grew. They had 17in x 24in cylinders, 140psi boiler pressure, 5ft wheels and weighed 36 tons. To 'beef' them up a bit Stirling rebuilt them with 17½in cylinders and a 150psi boiler pressure. No. 31, built in 1885, retains the Kirtley cab, but is otherwise as rebuilt. All ten were withdrawn by 1922.

Stirling's F2 class 0-6-2 coal tanks were equal to the best of the contemporary South Wales equivalents when introduced in 1901. Indeed, they lasted longer as, although scrapping began in 1936, the last ones survived until 1960. They had 18in x 26in cylinders, 175psi boiler pressure, 4ft 6in driving wheels, 23,197lbs T.E. and weighed 58 tons. No. 109 is at Springhead shed, Hull.

The twelve 0-6-0T engines of G1 class, designed by Kirtley and built 1884–5, were virtual copies of designs for his other employer, the LCDR. They had 17in x 24in cylinders and 140psi boiler pressure, about par for the day. No. 3, again at Springhead shed, was later sold to the Ashington Coal Co. in Durham, virtually in original condition.

Stirling's G3 class 0-6-0T, No. 113, rests in the all-too-familiar surroundings of Springhead shed. These five engines, built in 1901, had 18in x 26in cylinders, 175psi boiler pressure, 4ft 6in wheels, 23,197lbs T.E. and weighed 47 tons 7cwt. They were much better than earlier designs, the last ones surviving until 1960. The HBR engines suffered a similar fate to those of the Scottish railways absorbed by the LMS. Of the 181 that were passed onto the NER in 1922, only 138 made it into the LNER the following year, and only twelve to BR in 1948; quite a slaughter. None were to survive for preservation.

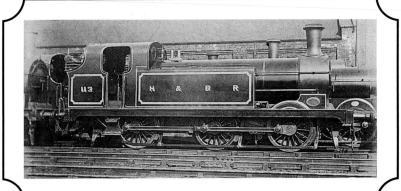

Midland Railway

Beginning life in 1844, following an amalgamation of the Midland Counties Railway, North Midland Railway and the Birmingham & Derby Junction Railway, all of which were centred on Derby, the MR expanded and acquired other companies, until it became the third largest railway in Britain. That it did not set out, unlike the GNR and LNWR, to link large cities and towns to London, but was more of a regional company, even after the 1844 amalgamation, makes its later rise to greatness all the more remarkable.

Expansion was both rapid and sustained, and continued until the eve of World War One. None other than the 'Railway King' himself, George Hudson, was the first Chairman and, as one would expect, he quickly began buying other companies. The Leicester & Swannington, dating to 1830 and thus becoming the oldest constituent of the MR, the Birmingham & Gloucester, and the broad gauge Gloucester & Bristol railways were all speedily acquired. It was while trying to purchase railways in Yorkshire that suspicion was aroused regarding the 'King's' activities; he was both buyer and seller!

Through traffic from the ever-growing towns of Derby, Nottingham, Leicester, Sheffield and Leeds, was carried to London via Rugby and the LNWR. The MR was thus in danger of becoming a 'feeder' railway, and its trains were often held up en route to Euston. So, in the 1850s the MR pushed south from Leicester – Bedford, and connected with the GNR at Hitchin, to allow access for its trains into King's Cross; the MR thus had two routes to London for its expanding passenger and goods traffic.

Any thoughts of competition improving the service MR London-bound trains received, did not last long. Horror stories of both its passenger, and goods, trains being delayed by the hour on the GNR and LNWR lines, abounded. They were probably fairly accurate as well, as after five years the MR sought, and obtained, Parliamentary permission to build its own line into London, from Bedford. This, and the magnificent, palatial, combined passenger and goods station at St Pancras, was opened in 1868. The MR had 'arrived' in style.

The year before had seen the MR route to Manchester, via Matlock, opened, and its one third owned, along with the GNR and MSLR, Cheshire Lines Committee route to Liverpool begin operations. One major link still remained to be exploited though, especially for a railway harbouring such grand ambitions; its own route to Scotland. Already owning various lines in the West Riding of Yorkshire, the MR pushed north from Settle to the border city of Carlisle. Running agreements were made with the G&SWR and the NBR to take expresses forward to Glasgow and Edinburgh respectively, beginning in 1876. The MR now moved up into the top league of railways.

Further acquisitions took the MR into South Wales, Ireland and finally, in 1912, it bought the LTSR. New lines were built to York, between Chinley and Sheffield, and numerous other smaller links; and to go with its part-ownership of the CLC, it jointly purchased the MGNJtR, with the GNR, and the Somerset & Dorset Railway, with the LSWR. Thus, by 1912, although not the largest railway by route mileage, the MR was the only railway to operate in all four home countries, including acquisitions and through workings. It also had its own 'sphere of influence', centred on Derby, with lines radiating in all directions.

Much of this drive to expand was due to the energies of James Allport. He joined the MR from the MSLR, in 1853, as General Manager, and for the next 27 years exerted an increasing dominance on company policy, either from a managerial position, or the boardroom. Unlike Edward Watkin, or indeed George Hudson, Allport was a 'one company', and especially 'Midland', man through and through. His commercial ambitions were directed through, and by, the MR. Of course, he was aided by an ever-growing workforce, one which had an increasing pride in the company, and seemed eager to establish 'Midland' traditions. This 'pride' was most obviously seen in the usually immaculate conditions of MR coaches and engines, even at a time when standards of appearance were high anyway, on other railways.

One MR tradition was 'light and fast', regarding the running of its trains. This affected both express and secondary trains and, most importantly, locomotive design. Matthew Kirtley was the first Locomotive Superintendent, who retired in 1873. He was responsible, in many ways, for establishing Derby Works with an excellent reputation for quality of build. The first engines were built there in 1851, and from then on its reputation grew. Kirtley's engines, as can be seen, were neither big nor powerful, but they were good runners, and were more than capable of carrying out the work demanded of them.

Samuel Johnson was appointed from the GER to replace Kirtley, and his designs followed the path laid down by both his predecessor, and Allport. Johnson designed some 4-4-0s early on, and these epitomised MR passenger services for many years to come: lightweight, fast, reliable and extremely handsome. These 4-4-0s grew steadily in size over the years, but were never particularly powerful. Unlike many other railways, the MR was not afraid of double-heading its trains; indeed it often seemed as though it preferred to.

Richard Deeley replaced Johnson, in 1903, and developed Johnson's last design, a compound 4-4-0.

These fine engines were the ultimate development of the MR 4-4-0, and were even built, little modified, in greater quantities, by the succeeding LMS. Deeley made way for Henry Fowler, in 1909, but had already begun the task of rebuilding, and modifying, many of Johnson's earliest designs. Deeley's and Fowler's own designs were virtual developments of Johnson's, and were constrained by the dictum 'light and fast', hence there was little need for massive building programmes. However, the continuity of design, from one Locomotive Superintendent to another, was unmatched by any other railway.

Thus, on the eve of World War One, the MR was indeed a powerful operator of railways. A steady continuity of growth and tradition made the MR a great favourite amongst regular passengers, and a company that its workers were proud to be associated with. Though perhaps steeped in tradition, the MR had always been quite innovative, particularly with regard to passenger comforts, like the upgrading of third class travel, and its mix of these qualities gave the MR its pre-eminent position among Edwardian British railways.

The advent of sanding gear in the 1880s, brought 'singles' back into fashion for express trains. After successfully designing 4-4-0s for many years, S. W. Johnson built his first single for the Midland Railway in 1887, followed by 94 more before retirement. They were mainly used on expresses south of Derby/ Nottingham, but also on the Bristol line, and were capable of speeds over 80mph with the lightly loaded trains of the time. No. 4, built in 1892, of 25 class, and No. 118, built in 1896, of the 115 class, and now preserved, make a splendid sight heading a typical express through Mill Hill. The 115 class had 19$\frac{1}{2}$in x 26in cylinders, 170psi boiler pressure, 7ft 9in driving wheels, 15,350lbs T.E. and weighed 47 tons. The class was finally withdrawn in 1928. No. 4 became No. 640, and No. 118 became No. 673 in the 1907 renumbering.

The 25 class 4-2-2s were the most numerous of Johnson's singles, 60 being built between 1887 and 1893. They had 18$\frac{1}{2}$in x 26in cylinders, 160psi boiler pressure, 7ft 6in driving wheels, 14,000lbs T.E. and weighed 44 tons with just 17$\frac{1}{2}$ tons for adhesion. Like all Johnson's singles, these were free steamers, but were usually lightly worked, due to MR loading policies. This picture of No. 1871, built in 1891, seen at Kentish Town, is dated 1900 and shows the fireman busy at work on the tender, while his driver waits in the cab. The engine is in the same position as a well-known picture of this engine. It was renumbered No. 628 in 1907.

Johnson's first design of single was the 1853 class. They were basically the same as the later 25 class, but had 7ft 4in driving wheels. No. 1859, built in 1889, and seen here at Kentish Town, was renumbered No. 616 in 1907. Johnson's singles were popularly known as "Spinners", due to their smooth running at speed, and the silent slipping of the driving wheels. Unlike their GNR counterparts, these were still hauling Leeds/Bradford expresses, usually as a pilot, into the 1920s.

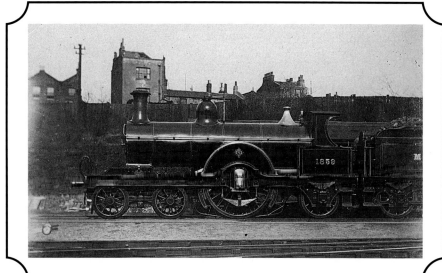

The 5.10pm from St. Pancras, approaches Childs Hill at speed behind 800 class No. 151A. Forty-eight of these 2-4-0s, designed by M. Kirtley, were built in 1870–1 at Derby and by Neilson. They had 17in x 24in (later 18in) cylinders, 140psi boiler pressure, 6ft 9in (later 6ft 7in) driving wheels, 11,000lbs T.E. and weighed 36 (later $40^{1}/_{2}$) tons. Initially, the 800 class worked all over the MR, but they were soon rebuilt by Johnson between 1875–82.

They subsequently performed admirably on the Anglo-Scottish services for many years, and were popular with drivers as they could be pushed very hard. No. 151A became No. 110 in 1907, and was withdrawn in 1930. A total of 121 Kirtley-designed 2-4-0s were passed onto the LMS at Grouping, the last of the 800 class not being withdrawn until 1936.

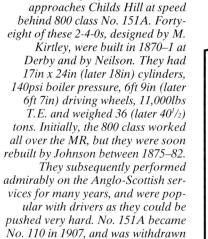

Johnson's initial designs of 2-4-0 were not obviously better than Kirtley's. However, his 1400 class, of which 60 were built between 1878 and 1881, proved to be excellent engines. They had 18in x 26in cylinders, 140psi boiler pressure, 6ft 9in driving wheels, 13,000lbs T.E. and weighed 41 tons, with 27 tons for adhesion. Initially used on London–Leeds expresses, they later worked Leeds–Morecambe/Furness services. As train weights increased, many of these were regularly used as 'pilots' on expresses, well into this century. No. 1481, built in 1880, and renumbered No. 231 in 1907, rests at Kettering before the day's work, judging by the driver's white shirt and clean waistcoat. One hundred and forty-four of Johnson's 2-4-0s entered LMS stock.

No. 1316, built in 1876, of the 1312 class, the first of eleven classes of Johnson 4-4-0, numbering 361 engines, built between 1876 and 1901, is at Liverpool Exchange, its home base. It became No. 304 in 1907, but this initial class was not a great success, deemed no better than the 2-4-0s. They had 17½in x 26in cylinders, 140psi boiler pressure, 17½ sq ft grate, 6ft 6in driving wheels, 13,000lbs T.E. and weighed 41 tons; dimensions enlarged steadily over the years.

The 20 engines of Johnson's 1740 class 4-4-0s, built 1885–7, were regarded as some of the best in the country when new. No. 1757 Beatrice, was the best known of these, and it is seen here at Kentish Town, in sparkling condition. It was exhibited at the Royal Jubilee Exhibition of 1887, opened by Princess Beatrice. In 1891 it was also used to haul the royal train, from London to Derby. The class had 18in x 26in cylinders, 160psi boiler pressure, 7ft driving wheels, 14,000lbs T.E. and weighed 43 tons, with 28 tons for adhesion. Renumbered No. 377 in 1907, it spent many years on the former LTSR lines, often working fast holiday trains from St Pancras after the MR took that company over.

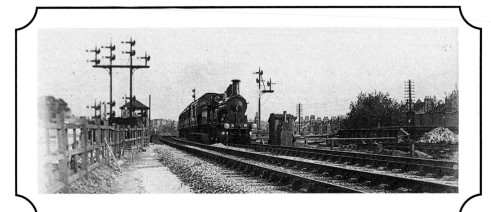

The 5pm St. Pancras–Leeds 'Diner' approaches Childs Hill, behind 4-4-0 No. 2429, of the 150 class, en route to its first stop, at Kettering. Lightly loaded expresses were the norm on the MR, and these were handled comfortably by Johnson's 4-4-0s, right into LMS days. This class was built between 1897 and 1900, and had 18½in x 26in cylinders, 160psi boiler pressure, 7ft driving wheels, 15000lbs T.E. and weighed 51 tons, with 38 tons for adhesion. This engine became No. 511 in 1907.

R. Deeley, on succeeding Johnson, began the task of updating many of his predecessor's early designs. No. 357, is shown at Manchester after being rebuilt with a larger boiler, the pressure being raised from 140 to 170psi, and with 7ft driving wheels. When rebuilt, Johnson's earlier designs performed as well as his later 4-4-0s, but the graceful lines gave way to more purposeful looks. This was formerly No. 1666, of 1562 class, built 1882–3.

The 2606 class, 'Belpaires', of 1900, were the definitive version of Johnson's 'simple' 4-4-0 designs. With $19^{1}/_{2}$in x 26in cylinders, 180psi boiler pressure, 6ft 9in driving wheels, 25 sq ft grate, 19,000lbs T.E. and weighing 53 tons, 38 tons for adhesion, these were the most powerful of that type, on the MR, by far. Built to reduce double-heading on the Settle–Carlisle route, they also competed against the GCR on long non-stop runs. The driver of the first 'Belpaire', No. 2606, checks over his engine, in the centre road of Carlisle Citadel station, before taking an express southwards. Eventually, the class numbered 80 engines, of which 22 survived onto British Railways books, the last being withdrawn in 1952.

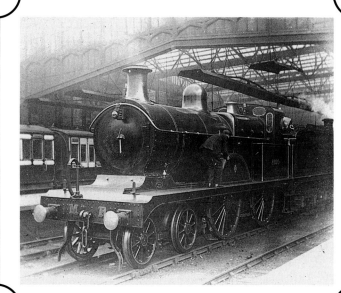

Deeley developed Johnson's 'compound' design, of 1901, itself influenced by the NER compounds rebuilt by Chief Draughtsman W. M. Smith, and eventually 45 were built. These originally had (2) 19in x 26in H.P. cylinders, (1) 21in x 26in L.P. cylinder, 195psi boiler pressure, 7ft driving wheels, 26 sq ft grate, 23,000lbs T.E. and weighed $59^{1}/_{2}$ tons for adhesion. Deeley's later engines differed slightly, having the very high 220psi boiler pressure and a $28^{1}/_{2}$ sq ft grate, along with other detail changes. These were particularly successful on the Settle–Carlisle and Peak District lines, but the light loading of MR passenger trains resulted in them being under-used. No. 1037, of the last batch from 1908/9, is at Manchester.

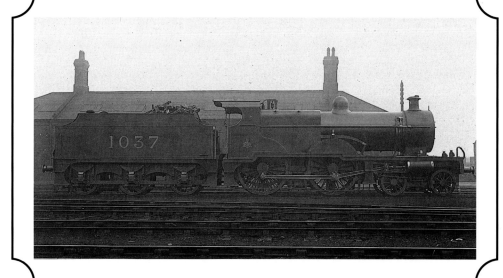

The six-month strike by members of the Amalgamated Society of Engineers, for the 8-hour working day, in 1897/8, is not usually regarded as being a 'success', but it certainly brought British engineering to a standstill. Railways began to look elsewhere for goods engines, and the MR bought 30 2-6-0s of the 2501 class from the Baldwin Co. of Philadelphia. These were sent over in crates and assembled at Derby, in 1899. Financially, they looked to be an attractive buy, costing £400 less than a British 0-6-0, with delivery within a year. However, in comparative tests with an 0-6-0, the Moguls used 20–25% more coal, 50% more oil, and needed 60% more time spending on repairs and maintenance. They had 18in x 24in cylinders, 180psi boiler pressure, 5ft driving wheels, 20,000lbs T.E. and weighted 45¾ tons, 37 tons for adhesion. They mainly worked Toton–London and Yorkshire coalfield based coal trains, and were quite popular with crews due to their large cabs. However, they were poor steamers, and an indifferent investment, as all were withdrawn by 1915. No. 2533, renumbered No. 2222 in 1907, partially hides a "Spinner" as it blows off steam at Kentish Town.

Johnson's goods engines proved to be a much better long term investment than the Baldwin Moguls, as hundreds were passed on to BR. No. 2268, later renumbered No. 3554, was built in 1897, but withdrawn after a mere 50 years. The 3460 class numbered 305 engines, built between 1894 and 1903, and had 18in x 26in cylinders, 175psi boiler pressure, 5ft 3in wheels, 20,000lbs T.E. and weighed 45 tons. No. 2268 is, again, standing at Kentish Town shed, nicely turned out.

Deeley's first goods engine design, the 3765 class of 1903–8, was an update of the earlier Johnson classes. Dimensions were identical to those of the engine in the previous picture, except for 21,000lbs T.E. and a weight of 44 tons. Many were used on the difficult Toton–London coal trains, but others led much easier lives, working on branch line duties. No. 3776, in a slightly dirty condition for the time, is loaded with coal and waiting for another duty at Manchester.

Several railway companies bought Beyer Peacock 4-4-0Ts, designed for use on London's underground. After electrification, these engines could be seen in many unexpected places. No. 206A, one of six built for the Metropolitan Railway in 1868, was sold to the MR for its Moorgate services. It had 17in x 24in cylinders, 120psi boiler pressure, 5ft 9in driving wheels, 11,000lbs T.E. and weighed 42 tons, with 31 tons for adhesion. They were all rebuilt in 1888, and cabs were added in 1900/1, when moved away from London. No. 206A is in this later condition at Lancaster, where it worked out its final years before withdrawal in 1904. Here is a fine view, showing the inclined cylinders and the condensing apparatus.

Kirtley designed the 690 class 0-4-4T for the underground services, and 26 were built in 1869-70. They had 17in x 24in cylinders, 140psi boiler pressure, 5ft 2¹/₂in driving wheels, 14,000lbs T.E. and weighed 50 tons, with 30 tons for adhesion. No. 786 became No. 1212 in 1907, and is at Kentish Town, after being rebuilt by Johnson. The condensing pipes and the sandbox on top of the boiler are clearly visible, and behind stands "Spinner" No. 1859, as depicted earlier. The class worked in and around London for over 50 years, with 25 engines being passed onto the LMS, some lasting into the 1930s.

Kirtley's 880 class tank No. 885A, built in 1871, passes Stratford with a goods train, in 1902 in a rather faded view. These attractive little engines, with half cabs, were another long serving class, although only ten were built. They had 16in x 24in cylinders, 140psi boiler pressure, 4ft 2in wheels, 15,000lbs T.E. and weighed 37 tons. No. 885A became No. 1616 in 1907.

On most railways 0-6-0Ts were expected to undertake a wide variety of duties, from shunting, to medium distance goods and even passenger trains. The 60 engines of Johnson's 1900 class, built between 1899 and 1902, were no exception to this dictum. They had 18in x 26in cylinders, 160psi boiler pressure, 4ft 7in wheels, 20,835lbs T.E. and weighed 49 tons. No. 2444, renumbered No. 1903 in 1907, is at Childs Hill with a goods train. Many engines of this class passed onto BR, and the LMS built a further 422 between 1924 and 1931, with only minor modifications.

In response to the increasing weight and speed of outer suburban trains around London, Birmingham and Manchester, Deeley designed the 2000 class, "Flatirons", in 1907. The 40 engines were quite powerful with 18½in x 26in cylinders, 175psi boiler pressure, 5ft 7in driving wheels, 19,750lbs T.E. and weighed 75½ tons, with 54 tons for adhesion, but were not exactly a success, though capable of running at over 60mph. After the MR took over the LTSR in 1912, six of these were sent to work there, but were not well received by crews and staff alike, not really being up to the job; they were soon despatched back. No. 2004 was one of those locomotives, and it is seen here at its original shed of Trafford Park, giving the impression of being hewn from the solid, rather than 'crafted' and created. Although later superheated and given a Belpaire firebox, the entire class was scrapped during the period 1935 to 1937.

London, Tilbury & Southend Railway

To generations of London's 'eastenders' the LTSR was known as the "Sarfend line"; the route of escape from the drudge of daily life, to the seaside. There was, and is, a certain popularity and attraction about Southend with its pier, beaches and its seeming resistance against moves to gentrify the town. That Southend had its own railway, upon which its growth depended, was only natural; both town and railway were quite different from 'genteel' Essex, and the GER, and both remained 'thorns' in their respective sides.

The London, Tilbury & Southend Extension Railway was, ironically, jointly promoted by the Eastern Counties Railway and the London & Blackwall Railway. It was opened to Tilbury, where an important connection was made with the Gravesend ferry, from Forest Gate, in 1854, the two miles from there into Fenchurch St. station being owned by the ECR. Two years later a line from Tilbury to Southend was completed, and the whole route was leased back to the contractors, and worked using ECR locomotives and stock.

In 1862 the LBR and ECR were absorbed into the new GER, but the LTSExtR remained independent, and changed its name to LTSR. The 'little brother' was very much the 'poor relation', and traffic remained light outside the rush hours, despite the running of excursions to Southend. That the LTSR was not absorbed by the GER during this period was probably due to the leasing arrangement. This was terminated in 1875, but instead of being drawn into the GER, the LTSR began to distance itself, bought its own locomotives and coaches, and planned the extension from Southend to Shoeburyness.

A. L. Stride became the Chairman in 1875, and remained in that post until the end. He was very much in the driving seat, and was determined to keep 'his' company out of the clutches of the GER. Competition from the GER increased with the opening of their own line to Southend, and so the Upminster cut-off, missing out Tilbury, was built, followed by branches from Upminster to Grays and Romford, to keep the GER at bay. Towards the end of the century, the MR began to run service trains and excursions to Southend from St Pancras, courting influence with the LTSR, while

relations with the GER were becoming somewhat cool. A not uncommon situation between railways in contemporary Britain.

From the 1880s traffic began to increase with the development of Southend, the building of Tilbury's ocean docks and particularly, the sprawl of London. Mr T. Whitelegg was appointed as Locomotive Superintendent in 1880, arriving with the first of the ubiquitous "TUMS" (Tilbury Universal Machines), his 4-4-2Ts from Beyer Peacock. That type of engine dominated the LTSR scene for both passenger and goods trains, right up until the end. His son, R. H. Whitelegg, took over in 1910, and in the two years that he held office, designed the first British Baltic, 4-6-4T engine. However, in 1912, out of 82 engines owned by the LTSR, 70 were "TUMS", and ten others were also tank engines. These "TUMS" were as much a part of the Tilbury's character, as the pier was of Southend's.

By early this century the LTSR was getting to be too big for its own shoes. Then, as now, congestion was causing delays, and the opening of further stations in the London area did not help in this matter either. Finances were always restricted and a likely solution to the over-crowding problems, electrification, was too expensive for the company; it looked to be only a matter of time before there was a merger with the GER. Then, in 1912, rather like a flirting daughter, the LTSR surprised everyone by 'jilting' the faithful, if occasionally estranged suitor, the GER, and ran off with the wealthy MR instead, with promises of riches, in the form of electrification, and accompanied by howls of protests from the Southend 'family'. The 'family' was appeased as the LTSR, though quickly subsumed by the MR, maintained its independence and character, to a degree, but it took 50 years for the promised electrification to arrive. By then, the former LTSR lines were embraced in the arms of the Eastern Region of BR, back where they started a hundred years before.

During its 60 years of independence, the LTSR blossomed into a railway that was warmly accepted as an essential part of everyday life for many people in South Essex. Its reputation among the East London workers was equally high, and the protests on losing its independence rang from all quarters. Little wonder the MR kept the system at arm's length.

Whitelegg's "TUMS", 4-4-2Ts were the mainstay of LTSR line services until the 1930s. The MR, and later the LMS, made several attempts to replace the "TUMS", but none of these were successful, until the advent of the Stanier 2-6-4Ts of 1934. One reason the "TUMS" held sway for so long, was the need to haul 12-coach outer suburban trains at an average speed of 50mph, not an easy task on the busy lines out of Fenchurch St. Hornsey Road *followed the tradition of naming the "TUMS" after stations of the line, and was a member of the 37 class, which numbered 34 engines built between 1897 and 1909. It is seen at Plaistow shed in this 1905 picture, with a Fenchurch St. headboard. They had 18in x 26in cylinders, 170psi boiler pressure, 6ft 6in driving wheels and weighed 71 tons, with 38 tons for adhesion.*

Sharp, Stewart built two 0-6-0s for the Ottawa Railway in 1898, which were never delivered. They were bought by the LTSR and one of them, No. 49, is at Plaistow with its crew, unusually, paying little attention to the photographer. Later on, both received a weather-shield on the tender to protect crews when running tender first, as the LTSR had few turntables. No. 49 became LMS No. 2898, and was scrapped during the 1930s.

London & North Western Railway

The ranks of railway enthusiasts and historians today certainly baulk at the title this company bestowed on itself: "The Premier Line". Using the usual measurements with which evaluations are made by these people, such as train speeds, power of locomotives, amount of route mileage and so forth, the LNWR did not deserve that title; in the first two cases it was well short of the mark. Remembering that, prior to 1948, railways were primarily businesses, such yardsticks are not necessarily appropriate. In the years leading up to World War One, the LNWR had the highest receipts of any railway company, and paid the highest dividends of the ten largest railways. Besides this, of the small band of contemporary enthusiasts, 'railwayacs', it is likely that the majority were ardent 'Crewe' supporters.

Of course, dividends influence the opinions of shareholders, just as high speeds impress enthusiasts. However, in terms of quality, and probably quantity, of services offered, the LNWR really was deserving of that prestigious title. This was, in the main, due to the Chairman, Sir Richard Moon, who held that post from 1861 until 1891, and had been employed by the LNWR for some years before. In many respects, he was fairly typical of the Victorian autocratic businessman, but he was worthy of being known as 'great', unlike so many others ascribed with that honour. With Moon as Chairman, receipts increased nearly threefold during a period of consistently falling prices, the so called 'Great Depression', and from 1865 onwards dividends were never lower than $6\frac{1}{4}\%$, this at a time when a 5% return was considered high. Moon's benchmark for the standards expected is best illustrated by his motto given to each new officer on his appointment:

"Remember first, that you are a gentleman; remember next, that you are a North Western officer, and that whatever you promise you must perform. Therefore, be careful what you promise, but having promised it, take care that you perform it."

To anybody who has studied British economic and social history, the origins of the LNWR will be all-too familiar. The world's first exclusively steam hauled passenger railway, the Liverpool & Manchester Railway, opened in 1830. This was followed by the London & Birmingham Railway, and the Grand Junction Railway, which connected the LMR and LBirmR via Crewe. The LBirmR and GJctR both obtained Acts of Parliament in 1833. Thus, from 1837 it was possible to travel by rail from London to the rapidly developing industrial areas of Lancashire.

In 1846, the GJctR, after taking over several other railways, including the LMR, amalgamated with the LBirmR, and Manchester & Birmingham Railway to form the LNWR. This new concern, with connections via the Lancaster & Carlisle Railway, and the opening of the CR route from Glasgow to Carlisle in 1848, gave a through route from London to Glasgow and Edinburgh, at a time when the GNR was still under construction.

Further amalgamations, takeovers and line building over the years, took the LNWR to Holyhead and North Wales, Swansea, the South Welsh 'valleys', Cambridge and Leeds. One takeover, that of the Sirhowy Railway in South Wales, in 1875, actually lengthened the LNWR ancestry. This began as a tramway in 1802, for the haulage of coal, and in 1829 the first steam engine, a six-wheeled type, was obtained. This was the 16th to be built at Stephenson's; *Rocket* being the 19th. Passengers were not carried until 1849, and it did not technically become a 'railway' until eleven years later.

In 1842 the GJctR opened the renowned works at Crewe, on virgin land; Wolverton was the home of the LBirmR Works. Francis Trevithick, son of Richard the man who built the first successful steam locomotive, was in charge at Crewe, although he was never an innovator like his father. His opposite number at Wolverton was J. E. McConnell, a much more forceful character, whose 'Bloomer' engines were both powerful and reliable.

John Ramsbottom took over from Trevithick in 1857, with something approaching a coup d'etat, and assumed total control with a similar manoeuvre against McConnell, in 1862. From that date, Wolverton became the carriage works, and all engines were built at Crewe. There was something ironic in this decision, as Crewe already had the reputation of building locomotives that were under-powered, unlike Wolverton; a tradition, or indeed indictment, which lasted until the closing years of the LNWR.

Ramsbottom did design some splendid engines, his 'Problem' and 'Newton' classes being versatile, long-lasting and reliable; very attractive to Moon and the shareholders. Speeds were not high on the LNWR, another Moon maxim that "40mph is the proper speed for a gentleman" (I wonder what Moon would have thought at modern BR trains being capable of $3\frac{1}{2}$ times that speed?) dictated running speeds; a regular and reliable service being more important. These engines fitted the bill perfectly.

Following Ramsbottom, in 1871, came Francis William Webb, a man whose autocratic stature and the enormous esteem in which he was held, was second only to Moon himself. For 32 years he was a virtual dictator at Crewe, and following Moon's retirement, seemingly of the whole company as well. In many respects his earlier engine designs, and rebuilding of Ramsbottom's engines, reflected Moon's opinions on economy and reliability.

In 1882 Webb turned to compounding for all his main locomotive designs, and it is from this time onwards that controversy surrounds his success as a locomotive engineer. Between that date and his retirement, Webb designed eight main passenger types, two classes for freight and one mixed traffic class, as compounds, none of which were fully masters of the work required of them. They were not particularly economical with fuel either, some being veritable coal eaters, and double-heading became rife on many expresses. It is not pleasant, but nevertheless necessary, to point out that George Whale, Webb's successor, immediately began the scrapping, or rebuilding as 'simples', of all of Webb's compounds. It is sad to reflect that, for all Webb's experimentation and persistence with compounding, none, with the exception of a few mixed traffic engines, survived the First World War.

There was to be no great technological change, with regard to locomotive matters, as happened on other railways with the dawning of the new century, new

fast-living monarch and new Locomotive Superintendent, like the MR, GWR and GCR. Whale's engines were very much in the LNWR mould of being reliable without the frills; in many respects like those of Webb, minus the compounding.

As has been suggested, the LNWR concentrated on giving service of the very highest class. Its passenger trains, like the colours carried, may not have been either the fastest, or the most flamboyant, but the quality, regularity and standard of service was second to none. Considering the size and wealth of the company, it did not pay its employees particularly well either. Yet the pride they took in their work suggests that there was more than a touch of the 'love affair' in the relationship. This was a railway that was held in a very special esteem in contemporary Britain, and reflected some of the better attributes of the Victorian era.

Unfortunately, the photographer took few panoramic pictures, and this one, of Edgeley Junction Stockport, only serves to show what has been missed. A LNWR 2-4-2T passes with a passenger train, while an 0-6-0 heads a goods train in the centre. On the left, a tank engine shunts in the sidings. The wide variety of wagons, the numerous signals and the general railway atmosphere, are evocative of an age when railways dominated life, like the motor car does today in a less than romantic situation.

Ramsbottom's second design for the LNWR was the celebrated 'Problem', or 'Lady of the Lake', class of which 60 engines were built between 1859 and 1865. Although relatively small, they worked expresses for over 20 years, and two were even brought off secondary duties to take part in the 1888 'races', to Edinburgh. They had 16in x 24in cylinders, 120psi (150psi as rebuilt) boiler pressure, 15 sq ft grate, 7ft 6in (7ft 9in) driving wheels and weighed 27 (31½) tons, with 11½ (14½) tons for adhesion. All were fully rebuilt by Webb, between 1895 and 1900. No. 117 Tiger, makes a lovely sight in this condition.

The 'Lady of the Lake' class had a distinguished career. At one time they hauled the longest non-stop run in the world, 103 miles from Holyhead to Crewe, and they were also the first engines to be able to collect water from troughs. Although unable to tackle expresses single handed-ly in the 1890s, they continued to work these as pilots, virtual-ly until the last one was with-drawn, in 1907. No. 610 Princess Royal, *built in 1862, is resplendent as she waits at Crewe.*

Ramsbottom's 'Samson' class 2-4-0, of which 50 were built 1863–6, and a further 40 between 1873 and 1879, were a bit on the small side by 1900. They had 16in x 20in cylinders, 120psi (later 150psi) boiler pressure, 6ft 1½in driving wheels and weighed 26 tons. However, No. 724 Eden, *from the earlier batch, makes a spirit-ed effort up the 1 in 90 out of Lancaster with the 5.27pm Windermere–Manchester express, watched by an admir-ing platelayer, and showing that after nearly 30 years service it could still 'do the business'.*

Webb's 'Precedent' class, of which 70 were built between 1874 and 1882, were similar to Ramsbottom's 'Newton' class. Known as "Jumbos", they had 17in x 24in cylinders, 140psi boiler pressure, 6ft driving wheels, 10,500lbs T.E. and weighed 33 tons, with 22 tons for adhesion. Designed to haul expresses south of Crewe, they remained on these services for over 30 years, despite many attempts to replace them. No. 2183 Antelope, *and No. 262* Wheatstone, *pass Bushey Troughs at high speed. These were both popular and success-ful engines, arguably Webb's finest. The last "Jumbo" was withdrawn in 1915.*

Webb's first compounds, the 'Experiment' class of 1882–4, was expected to replace the 'Precedents', but were sluggish engines. They had (2) 13in x 24in H.P. cylinders, (1) 26in x 24in L.P. cylinder, 150psi boiler pressure, 6ft 6in driving wheels, 13,500lbs T.E. and weighed 35 tons, with 27 tons for adhesion. Though quickly displaced off expresses by the 'Dreadnoughts', Webb still regarded these pioneers as being a success. No. 323 Britannic heads a Birkenhead train near Hooton, in its latter years. All were withdrawn by 1905.

By the 1890s Webb was firmly committed to compounding, and to cope with increased train loads, he designed the first 2-2-2-2 of the 'John Hick' class in 1894, with nine more built in 1898. They had two 15in x 24in H.P. cylinders, one 30in x 24in L.P. cylinder, 200psi boiler pressure, 6ft 3in driving wheels and weighed 52 tons, with 31 tons for adhesion. No. 1559 William Siemens is being turned at Liverpool Lime Street, a peculiarly elegant design. They were intended for use between Crewe and Carlisle, but were not particularly successful, often having to be double-headed on even the easy LNWR schedules. If longevity is an acceptable guide to the success and usefulness of a locomotive class, then these were the last of Webb's compounds to be scrapped, the final one going in only 1912.

Impressive though they looked on paper, engines of the 'John Hick' class were neither popular with their crews, nor successful on the Crewe–Carlisle expresses. Nevertheless, No. 1548 John Penn makes an impressive sight as it climbs Shap with an express, comprising six-wheeled coaches and a TPO. Some engines were later transferred to Shrewsbury, for the Hereford turns, prior to their early demise.

Despite mediocre success, Webb persevered with compounding, and in 1897 introduced his first 4-cylinder design, the appropriately named 'Jubilee' class. Forty engines were built by 1900, having two 15in x 24in H.P. cylinders, two 20½in x 24in L.P. cylinders, 175psi (later 200psi) boiler pressure, 7ft 1in driving wheels, 20,000lbs T.E. and weighing 55 tons, with 34 tons for adhesion. 'Experiment' No. 1102 Cyclops, pilots 'Jubilee' No. 1911 Centurion through Willesden, with the 2pm ex-Euston, "Scotch diner".

The 'Jubilees' were probably the most successful and popular of Webb's compound passenger engines. The last ones, although much rebuilt, survived until 1938, unlike many of Webb's designs. They were not fast downhill runners but, made up for this by being good hill-climbers, despite their large wheels. Certainly, they were well up to the tasks imposed by the "Premier Line" at the time, though often taking a pilot on expresses. No. 1917 Inflexible shows its simple lines, in front of a GWR engine.

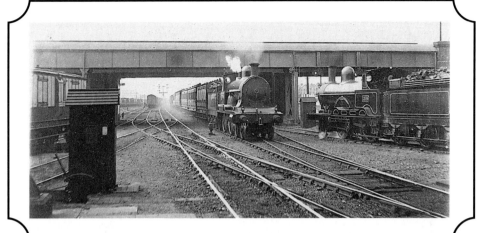

Webb's final compound passenger design, was the 'Alfred the Great' class, 40 examples being built 1901–3. No. 1943 Queen Alexandra *thunders through Willesden with an express due to arrive in Euston at 1.30pm. The engine waiting to pass onto the sheds is Ramsbottom's 'Newton' class, No. 1525* Abercrombie. *This class, of 96 engines, was very popular throughout its lifespan of over 30 years, the last ones being withdrawn in 1908.*

As with nearly all of Webb's compounds, the 'Alfred the Greats' were quickly displaced from the front rank expresses once the great man had retired. They were rebuilt, but then survived until 1928, when the last one was withdrawn. They had two 16in x 24in H.P. cylinders, two 20$\frac{1}{2}$in x 24 in L.P. cylinders, 200psi boiler pressure, 7ft 1in driving wheels, 20,000lbs T.E. and weighed 58 tons, with 37 tons for adhesion. No. 1955 Hannibal *hurries through Pinner and Hatch End with the 5.30pm express from Euston. The photographer's companion hides the platform furniture.*

Careful observation of No. 1850 of Webb's distinctive A class 3-cylinder compounds, will show the huge L.P. cylinder beneath the smokebox door. One hundred and eleven were built between 1893 and 1900 with two 15in x 24in H.P. cylinders, one 30in x 24in L.P. cylinder, 175psi boiler pressure, 4ft 5$\frac{1}{2}$in wheels, 30,000lbs T.E. and weighing 50 tons. Once Whale replaced Webb, rebuilding of these as 2-cylinder simples began in earnest, and all were thus converted by 1912. The last ones were withdrawn in 1931.

Proof that Webb's 2-4-2Ts worked all over the LNWR, is offered in this picture of 910 class No. 2128, at Cambridge. They had 17in x 24in cylinders, 160psi boiler pressure, 5ft 6in driving wheels, 14,500lbs T.E. and weighed 51 tons. Used mainly on branch and suburban workings, 160 were built between 1890 and 1897, with 38 fitted for push-pull duties.

The final ones were withdrawn in 1956, the last surviving passenger engines of Webb's design. Before heading west, the driver checks his engine, beside contemporary fire fighting equipment.

An unidentified 2-4-2T works a Broad St. 'Outer Circle' train past Mildmay Park. This offers a good view of a largish suburban station, at the turn of the century, with the fancy ironwork, and other features, synonymous with Victorian/Edwardian middle class England.

North London Railway

These photographs of the NLR, taken about 90 years ago, show the railway after its zenith, but before serious decline set in. If you were one of the thousands of daily passengers at that time, the all-round deprivation, not to say dereliction, of recent years would have been unimaginable. Somehow the main route has survived, and has lately even undergone some modernisation, but the loss of status can never be replaced, as the North London line is now just one of the many suburban routes out of Liverpool St. station.

Founded in 1846 as the East & West India Dock & Birmingham Junction Railway, building was slow to get started, as the 'railway mania' ran out of steam. The first service from Fenchurch St. – Islington began in 1850, with trains running at 15-minute intervals; operated by the London & Blackwall Railway. As soon as the connection with the LNWR was made at Camden, the latter company took over the running of the NLR; perfectly reasonable as it owned 70% of NLR capital stock. Again, that arrangement proved to be unsuitable and the NLR soon began to use its own coaches and engines.

With the opening of the North & South Western Junction Railway to Kew in 1853, and the later Hampstead line, traffic to the 'City' along the NLR grew rapidly. The need for its own 'City' terminus became desperate and Broad St. was opened, jointly with the LNWR, in 1865. The last NLR trains ran into Fenchurch St. three years later.

A further development took place with the opening of the Finsbury Park – Cannonsbury line by the GNR. This was intended to give the GNR both access to the docks, and also a 'City' station, at Broad St. The omnipotent LNWR would not entertain such a plan, so a compromise was reached whereby NLR trains worked onto the GNR suburban lines. When the new services were fully operative, Broad St. became the busiest London terminus during the rush hours.

By the 1880s there was a flood of trains leaving Broad St. every hour for Richmond, Kew, Watford, Willesden, Poplar and the various GNR destinations; all made up of four-wheeler coaches hauled by 4-4-0Ts. This lucrative business was soon to attract the attention of ominbus, underground and, later, tram companies. Passenger traffic began to wane during the 1890s, and diminished rapidly early this century, the crisis point being quickly reached. In 1909 the running of the NLR was taken over by the LNWR, but it remained independent and still had a board of directors. Economies of scale improved the financial position, although the loss of status was resented by staff.

The first Locomotive Superintendent had been none other than William Adams, 1854–73, later of the GER and LSWR. He designed the distinctive and efficient 4-4-0Ts on which the NLR depended for so many years. Adams' successors, J. C. Park, 1873-93 and H. J. Pryce, 1893–1908, updated the original designs to perpetuate these popular engines.

In many respects the NLR deserved its fate. During the 'fat' years of the last century high dividends were paid, at the expense of investment, and four-wheeler coaches were still being built in 1910. As always in such circumstances, it was the employees who suffered most. Those who kept their jobs lost their professional dignity and pride, and with that went the character of the line. Any form of redress is long overdue.

Another view of Mildmay Park station, this time showing Adams 4-4-0T No. 88 of the North London Railway, with a Broad St.–Enfield train. Mildmay Park, undergoing some repainting at that time, was opened in 1880, closed in 1934 and was the fourth out of Broad Street.

Adams designed these popular 4-4-0Ts of No. 1 class in 1868. They had 17in x 24in cylinders, 160psi boiler pressure, 5ft 6in driving wheels, 14,700lbs T.E. and weighed 43½ tons. Though later modified, these engines were the mainstay of NLR services for over 60 years. No. 31 passes the signal box, and a taxi office, as it enters Acton, later Acton Central, on the North and South Western Junction Railway.

Another picture of No. 88, built in 1898, with a GNR lines train at Hornsey, a favourite location of the photographer. In the background a Stirling 0-6-0ST is busy shunting. Cameras were fairly awkward and hefty things to carry around at this time, so the photographer needed to get a move on, as a train is passing under the signal gantry, on the line on which he is standing.

Adams designed these handsome 4-4-0Ts in 1863, for passenger work. They had 17in x 24in cylinder, 160psi boiler pressure, 5ft 9in (later 5ft 11in) driving wheels and weighed 42 tons, with 30 tons for adhesion. No. 113, seen here at Bow, wore the No. 16 until 1889, when it was rebuilt as seen, with a cab and it received a new boiler in 1890. No. 113, built in 1869, was scrapped in 1910, but several of the class survived until 1925.

These little 0-6-0Ts, designed by J. C. Park in 1879, for goods work, enjoyed lengthy lives, with 15 being passed on to BR, the last one working the Cromford–High Peak line until 1960, and is now preserved. They had 17in x 24in cylinders, 160psi boiler pressure, 4ft 4in wheels, 18,140lbs T.E. and weighed 44 tons. No. 78, built in 1882, is at Bow sheds and survived until the 1930s.

Lancashire & Yorkshire Railway

It has been said that the people of a country get the government they deserve; if that is true, then it would not just be modern day Britons who wonder what they have done to deserve the recent Tory governments. This saying is perhaps more accurate when applied to the pre-Grouping railway companies, concerning the areas they served: the hard working Welsh valleys and their busy little railways; the rural and grandiose South served by the LBSCR; and the "muck an' brass" areas of industrial Lancashire and the West Riding of Yorkshire, and the LYR. These two regions, separated by the daunting 'backbone of England', were the centre of the Industrial Revolution. Unchecked building, and a massive population growth, led to a life-style, for the vast majority, of untold misery, a desperate struggle for daily survival, and pollution on a scale unheard of even today; can you imagine seven tons of soot falling each year on a square mile near your house?

This was the land of the LYR. Goods traffic contributed well over half of turnover each year this century, and short haul passenger traffic added most of the rest; no fancy Pullmans and business expresses here. Like many of the larger businesses based in these two areas, the LYR thrived on its surroundings. In terms of route mileage, the LYR was very much a 'third division' railway, and yet, when measured by most other criteria, such as number of locomotives, turnover, dividends paid and so on, it was very much in the 'second division', and often well to the fore. In

terms of turnover per route mile, the LYR was ahead of any railway with more than 100 route miles.

The very title adopted by the amalgamation of the Manchester & Leeds Railway and five others in 1847, of LYR was arrogant and showed a determination to succeed. What other venture so obviously links these two counties, often personifying the term 'enemy', together – could you imagine a Lancashire and Yorkshire Cricket Club, for example? In the early years, the LYR certainly displayed plenty of arrogance towards its passengers, and especially those who travelled third class. The trains were unreliable, slow and unkempt, while the coaches, for all classes, were some of the poorest around; many stations were also appalling for the time. Indeed, for much of the last century, the LYR was regarded as the worst railway in Britain; this reputation could have been much worse had it served London, and not remained in the North, beyond the glare of national publicity.

The LYR expanded steadily throughout the nineteenth century, fairly dominating Lancashire between Preston and Manchester/Liverpool, and more than holding its own in the general mêlée of railways in the West Riding. Running powers were widely used and access was gained by these to York, Doncaster, Leeds, Hull and eventually even London, via the GCR and Sheffield. The through trains were the 'stars of the show', but one has to say, that were it not for having a captive audience, the LYR might well have been playing to an empty hall.

By the time serious competition arrived, in the form of the motor vehicle, the LYR had put its house in order and was up alongside the best railways in Britain. From the mid-1870s onwards, Britain's position in terms of world industrial power, was on the way down. One of the standard reasons given for this 'entrepreneurial decline', a supposed lack of business motivation among the capitalists. Fortunately, for the LYR, George Armytage, formerly a director and standing Vice-Chairman, did not suffer this trait when appointed Chairman, in 1887. There he remained for 31 years and, thanks to his ambition and efforts, the LYR was transformed into a railway worthy of its title.

Massive capital expenditure, including the new works at Horwich, up-grading the trackbed over many routes, rebuilding stations, new locomotives and coaches, was essential to raise the standard of service. The spirit of enterprise thrived with the opening of the company's docks at Fleetwood, and the purchase of the Goole Steamship Co. and the Co-operative (CWS) fleet, both based at Goole, by 1906. Services were run to Holland, Belgium, France, Denmark and Germany, and the LYR had the largest shipping fleet of any British railway company. Innovations, particularly the development of excursion traffic to huge proportions, encouraged rather than discouraged travel by the 'masses', adding to the already healthy profits. Dividends remained good, at between 4 and 5% pa, until Grouping, and the directors and shareholders felt happier with the improved reputation of 'their' railway.

The locomotive stock tended to reflect the contemporary standing of the LYR, at any given time. The first two consultant engineers, Messrs J. Hawkshaw, and Jenkins, followed by the first Locomotive Superintendent, Mr W. Hurst, provided engines of poor quality, including large numbers of 'singles'. Mr W. Barton-Wright, who was appointed in 1876, rationalised and scrapped most of his unfortunate inheritance, and also ordered many new engines from outside builders. His most lasting achievement, before leaving for India after ten years, was the planning of the new works at Horwich.

John Aspinall was appointed, from the GtSWR, and having had the first engine built at Horwich, in 1889, set about standardising the stock. He also designed a thoroughly modern fleet of engines, capable of taking the LYR into the 20th century. Uniquely among British Locomotive Superintendents, Aspinall became the General Manager, and was replaced by Mr H. A. Hoy in 1899. During his five years in office, Hoy continued very much in the same vein as Aspinall, multiplying successful designs. George Hughes was the last incumbent, and his engine designs were built to massive proportions, and imposing strength. They were certainly purposeful, if not exactly fleet of foot, and were ideally suited to the difficult terrain, north and east of Manchester. He became the first Chief Mechanical Engineer of the LMS, after Grouping.

The fortunes of the LYR seemed to reflect those of the people in the areas it served, rather than the national status. In the few decades of the last century when Britain was 'Great' in industrial terms, the LYR was in as poor a condition as were most people living nearby. Later, as Britain was being caught up, and then overtaken, by the USA and Germany, but conditions for ordinary working people began to improve, so the fortunes of the LYR rose. The bold step of increasing capital investment, during the Great Depression, was justly rewarded both financially, and with a greatly enhanced reputation. The LYR eventually received its reward for being as 'bold as brass'.

Aspinall's '978' class 4-4-0s were similar to those designed by Barton-Wright, his predecessor on the Lancashire & Yorkshire Railway. They began life on trans-Pennine expresses, and continued in that role for over 20 years. Although displaced from those duties as larger engines appeared, many survived into the 1930s working secondary lines. They had 18in x 26in cylinders, 160psi (later 180psi) boiler pressure, 6ft driving wheels and weighed 43³/₈ tons, many later received Belpaire fireboxes. No. 996, built in 1888 by Beyer Peacock, is waiting to depart Leeds Central with a Lancashire bound express.

No. 452, built in 1901, and rebuilt as early as 1908, enjoyed a lengthy life. It became LMS No. 12429, and later BR No. 52429, being scrapped in 1960. A member of Aspinall's 11 class, built between 1889 and 1909 with only minor modifications, it is seen here in original condition. They had 18in x 26in cylinders, 160psi (later 180psi) boiler pressure, 5ft 1in wheels, 21,130lbs T.E. and weighed 42 tons 3 cwt. A typical example of a traditional British goods engine.

No. 1054 was one of the first of Aspinall's 11 class to be built, in 1890. It was rebuilt in 1910, and became LMS No. 12096, but was scrapped in 1934. It is seen here accelerating past Rainford Junction, with a goods train, from Liverpool. The LNWR lines veer away to the left of the imposing signal box, offering a sight once so common throughout Britain, and sadly missed today.

Furness Railway

The FR was incorporated in 1844 to connect some iron ore mines near Kirkby and Dalton, to the coast at Barrow, in that part of Lancashire situated on the Cumbrian peninsula. This was an isolated concern, and its first engines had to be brought in by sea.

A year later, the Whitehaven & Furness Junction Railway began to build from Whitehaven to connect with the FR, and by 1850 there was a direct coastal link from Carlisle to Barrow. A few years later the through line from the LNWR at Carnforth, via Barrow and Whitehaven, was completed.

At that time, due to the FR, Barrow was growing very rapidly indeed, giving the railway influence, prestige and, importantly, profits. This, in turn, encouraged expansion and in the next decade, the FR connected up with the MR 'Little North Western' line at Wennington, and amalgamated with the WFJctR.

However, its die had been cast, the FR was as dependant on Barrow, and its continued growth, as was the town on the FR. The FR was hemmed into the Cumbrian peninsula, and even confined to the bottom half, as nine other railway companies, not all built to 'standard gauge', operated west of the LNWR West Coast Main Line. Demand for haematite grew in the 1870s, creating more traffic, and attempts were made to develop Coniston and Windermere as tourist attractions. Success in these fields was limited and it was the carriage of ores, the continued development of Barrow and local traffic, that provided a steady stream of dividends, and ensured independence, until Grouping.

Locomotive needs were modest, in both quantity and capacity; this is best illustrated by the 1840's engine "Coppernob", surviving in service until 1900. Prior to R. Mason being appointed as Locomotive Superintendent in 1890, all engines were bought 'off the shelf' from outside builders. W. F. Pettigrew took over in 1897 and he produced modern, if not especially inspired, designs, all still built elsewhere.

The FR was, like many British railway companies, never important outside its area of operation, but was nonetheless a consistent dividend payer. As happened all over Britain in the days before World War One, the combination of local esteem, a little competition and pride in one's work encouraged the smaller railways not only to remain independent, but to show they could out-do their larger rivals.

Such was the case with the FR which eschewed the advances of certain larger suitors, with designs on the profit potential of Barrow. As with that proverbial question, 'what came first, the chicken or the egg?' so one could ask the same of the FR and Barrow. This is one for the local historians to sort out, but the shareholders of the FR were not about to abandon the town, nor the town its railway.

All Furness Railway locomotives were constructed by outside builders, but were proudly maintained at Barrow. Mason's K2 class was virtually a 'stock' Stephenson design, and six were purchased in 1896, followed by two more, from Sharp, Stewart, in 1900. They had 18in x 26in cylinders, 160psi boiler pressure and 6ft driving wheels, being intended for passenger duties. No. 22, of the Stephenson batch, became LMS No. 10138, and was withdrawn in 1928. It is seen at Carnforth, displaying the classical lines of a British 4-4-0.

W. Pettigrew had worked under W. Adams on the GER and the LSWR, and some of the latter's influence can be seen in this picture of K3 class No. 126. Four engines to this design were purchased from Stephenson in 1900–1 for passenger duties. They were a great improvement on previous designs, and were capable of over 60mph on the short stretches between stations. They had 18in x 26in cylinders, 160psi boiler pressure and 6ft 6in driving wheels. No. 126 became LMS No. 10143, and was withdrawn in 1931. She makes a fine sight at Carnforth, when nearly new.

One of the more unusual facets of the FR, was its retention of the 'Bury' type 0-4-0 for goods trains. The last engines of this type built were the A5 class, of 1865, and No. 28, built by Stephenson in 1866, was not withdrawn until 1918. The large copper firebox, though not as prominent as on the preserved "Coppernob", stands out, and only modest weather protection is offered to the crew, as it busies itself at Barrow.

North Staffordshire Railway

The NSR was something of an enigma among the pre-Grouping railways. Hemmed in by the giants LNWR and MR, with the GWR, GNR and GCR all throwing in their twopennyworth of influence, this popular little railway, the 'Knotty', defied all commercial logic and not only survived, but flourished, until swallowed up by the LMS.

Formed by an amalgamation of the Newcastle & Sandbach, Churnet Valley, and Potteries railway companies in 1845, it became the Churnet Valley & Trent Junction Railway, and later the NSR. The system was centred on Stoke-on-Trent, and was made up of a cross between the Macclesfield – Colwich/Norton line, and Crewe/Sandbach – Eggington Junction line which connected with the LNWR and MR respectively. Later additions, in the 1860s, enhanced route mileage and offered connections with the GWR at Market Drayton, the MSLR (later GCR) to the north and the GNR Nottingham–Stafford/Burton services, which used NSR lines. Two further additions are worthy of note. The 'loop' line, from Etruria–Kidsgrove in the 'Five Towns' area, was renowned nationally thanks to Arnold Bennett's novels, and was opened in 1875. Finally, the commercially naive, 2ft 6in gauge Leek & Manifold Railway, was opened in the foothills of the Peak District in 1905.

Conflict, of one kind or another, was never far away, and the NSR became quite adroit at avoiding any serious consequences. Even at the outset it managed to circumvent a potential, financially damaging contretemps with the powerful Trent & Mersey Canal, by offering shares to the latter. Later confrontations with the 'Goliath' LNWR, over the routeing of certain London–Manchester expresses via Stoke, resulted in the 'David' NSR being successful, and still remaining independent. Finally, the way in which it neatly sidestepped any 'sanctions', and retained mutual working arrangements with the MR, LNWR and GNR, over access to the lucrative beer traffic at Burton-on-Trent, was more reminiscent of Talleyrand at the Congress of Vienna in 1815.

Train services were dominated, from the outset, by the need to make connections elsewhere. The routeing of certain Manchester–London and Manchester–Birmingham expresses, via Stoke, gave the NSR a main line character. Through services, with the GNR and GCR, further ensured the NSR did not remain a sleepy backwater. In 1900, Stoke had about 230 trains calling daily, with very few originating or terminating there.

Stoke also had its own works, opened in 1868. Mr W. Angus was the Locomotive Superintendent, until 1876, followed by L. Clare, to 1882 and Luke Longbottom, until 1902. These last two produced engines worthy of a far more important railway; the NSR enginemen never felt inferior to the LNWR counterparts when taking the Manchester – Stoke portions of the expresses. Indeed, it may well have been the LNWR enginemen who looked wistfully at the graceful, fleet of foot and economical NSR engines, as they nimbly and enthusiastically steamed out of Manchester London Rd station. There was no need to thrash these little ladies just to keep time.

Obviously a proud railway, the NSR was more than just a 'survivor'. Despite serious competition in its heartland around the Potteries from trams, it never failed to pay a dividend to the shareholders. This, and loyalty among both workers and customers, is a sure sign of a successful company. To be subsumed into a vast, often impersonal concern, like the LMS, was scant reward for 80 years of spirited existence, when it could often 'cock a snook' at its mighty neighbours. Ultimately, they rather unceremoniously 'had their day' at the expense of their 'cheeky' little rival.

In 1882 the North Staffordshire Railway built more of L. Clare's C class 2-4-0s to haul the London–Manchester expresses. These four engines performed this prestigious duty for over 20 years and were, naturally, worked with enthusiasm by the crews. They had 16½in x 24in cylinders, 140psi boiler pressure, 6ft driving wheels, and were thorough masters of the job. No. 55 Colin Minton Campbell, *built in 1882 at Stoke, is seen at Macclesfield. It was withdrawn in 1911, a short life for its day.*

Mersey Railway

This was another of those 'small is beautiful' railways that abounded in Britain, until 1923. With about five route miles, the Mersey Railway was one of the smallest standard gauge railways anywhere. Yet, with its own locomotives and coaches, it performed a very useful service, and even sprang to national prominence when, in 1903, it became the first steam railway in Britain to adopt electric traction.

Despite being incorporated to connect Birkenhead with Liverpool, by means of a tunnel under the River Mersey in 1866, the Mersey Tunnel Railway, as it was originally known, did not open until 1886. Within a year it was in the hands of the Receiver and, with falling passenger figures, the future looked bleak. A year later the Mersey Railway connected with the newly opened Wirral Railway, at Birkenhead Park station, which offered a life-line to both companies.

That was followed in 1891, by an equally important extension, to connect with the joint LNWR/GWR line at Rock Ferry, and later by building from James St. to a new Low Level station at Liverpool Central. In 1898 a through service from Paddington–Liverpool Central L.L. was begun, giving the MerR a taste of the 'big time'. Services between Liverpool and Rock Ferry/Birkenhead Park were frequent, and reasonably well patronised, and the future seemed secure. However, with gradients as steep as 1 in 27, the line was difficult to work, and extremely unpleasant for both passengers and engine crews, in the tunnels. So, in 1900, the brave decision to electrify the railway was taken.

The MerR eventually owned 21 steam locomotives, built and designed by outside suppliers. These were all sold following electrification, the last being disposed of in 1907. Though regular passengers may not have believed it, they were all fitted with condensing apparatus, but the steep gradients ensured that a completely smoke-free journey was seldom undertaken.

Once the big step to electrify had been taken, the railway guaranteed both its future, and its independence. A remarkable achievement considering the inauspicious beginnings.

The Mersey Railway also bought two 4-4-0Ts from the Metropolitan Railway, to act as service locomotives. Here, No. 2, enshrouds itself in steam, while standing at Birkenhead Central. It was built by Beyer Peacock in 1864, and became Metropolitan No. 7. The Mersey later sold this engine back to the Metropolitan, and it was rebuilt, for a second time, in 1921, and finally scrapped eight years later.

The Mersey Railway needed powerful locomotives as it was an awkward, steeply-graded line, with gradients up to 1 in 27. Nine 0-6-4Ts were bought from Beyer Peacock in 1885/6, and No. 1 The Major, was the first to be delivered. They had 21in x 26in cylinders (the largest in Britain at the time), 150psi boiler pressure, 4ft 7in driving wheels and weighed 67 tons 17cwt. After electrification, The Major was sold to J. A. Brown of New South Wales, in 1907. Fortunately, No. 5 Cecil Raikes has been preserved.

Wirral Railway

Considering this was such a small railway, it contrived to have quite a complicated history. Its ancestry can be traced to the incorporation of the Hoylake Railway in 1863, opening between Hoylake and Birkenhead Docks in 1866. Permission was granted to extend to Seacombe, New Brighton and West Kirby, but this section was never built, and the whole line closed after only four years.

At that time of rapid population growth, the middle classes were moving away from the industrial centres, and the Wirral peninsula was becoming a popular 'escape' for the wealthy people of Liverpool. Hence, the line re-opened after two years, partly as a tramway, but still led a precarious existence.

The WR was incorporated in 1883, and lines from Birkenhead Park and Docks–New Brighton were opened in 1888. Three years later a new WR was formed through amalgamations, while the line to West Kirby, and the Birkenhead Joint Railway opened. Further connections with the Wrexham, Mold & Connah's Quay (later GCR), and the Mersey Railway at Birkenhead Park, gave the WR through workings.

Though small in scale, the WR operated a comprehensive timetable and, in 1905, even more services were offered, which included a through train to Manchester. The growth of the number of people living on the Wirral, who worked in Liverpool, had benefited the WR enormously, and New Brighton was being developed as a resort.

Eric Barker was the first Locomotive Superintendent, until 1902, and his various tank engine designs, though restricted, were noteworthy performers. Most worked dual roles, passenger and goods, quite happily and efficiently. T. B. Hunter then took over the post until Grouping, and essentially carried on in the same vein, there being little need for extravagant spending on engines. All of these were quickly withdrawn by the LMS.

That the company remained independent until 1923, despite being surrounded by the LNWR, GWR and GCR, says something about the desire of the final WR to survive. After the earlier humiliations, this was probably its most lasting epitaph.

E. G. Barker designed two 0-6-4Ts, built by Beyer Peacock in 1900, for goods and excursion traffic on the Wirral Railway. They had 18in x 26in cylinders, 170psi boiler pressure, 5ft 2in driving wheels and 18,550lbs T.E. No. 15 is busy working at Birkenhead, with two guards vans, and a shunter in attendance. It was withdrawn in 1923/4.

East & West Junction Railway

This was the senior partner of three minor railways that amalgamated in 1903, to form the equally insignificant Stratford-on-Avon & Midland Junction Railway. A further amalgamation, with the Northampton & Banbury Junction Railway, two years later, did not improve matters. It was rather like all the decrepit railways of the Midlands being cast together in an asylum; an 'untouchable' which none of its major neighbours wanted to be associated with.

Founded in 1864 to build from the GWR, at Stratford, to the NBJctR, near Towcester, the line took nine years to complete, even though it was single track. It was engineered by Thomas Crampton, of locomotive design fame, and lack of finance was a problem from the outset. Within two years, it was in the hands of the Receiver, and in 1877 passenger services were suspended for eight years. One peculiarity was that the EWJctR operated all trains on the neighbouring Evesham, Redditch & Stratford-on-Avon Railway, while having no passenger trains of its own. That poor wretch of a railway was also in the hands of the Receiver by 1886; all the bad-eggs together in one basket.

The EWJctR was originally built to carry iron ores from Northamptonshire to the new South Wales iron works. Unfortunately, cheaper Spanish ores were used from the beginning, and so the expected traffic did not materialise. Only two engines were owned in the early days, and the whole railway had an air of 'doom and gloom' about it. In 1899 a connection was made with the GCR, at Woodford Halse, and a limited, but important, amount of through traffic was generated. Until then, only a few elderly engines worked the line, but the heavier GCR coaches required larger engines, all purchased from outside builders. Traffic remained light however, and by the time of the amalgamation, the EWJctR was merely the biggest fish in a very small pond.

The survival instinct seems to have been very strong in all four companies that formed the SMJctR. All had been in the hands of the Receiver, and yet the line flourished during World War One. This was the one highspot in its history, and afterwards it returned to its sleepy, precarious existence.

The last 2-4-0 engine built for a British railway, was the East & West Junction Railway No. 13, by Beyer Peacock in 1903. It was similar to the HBR 2-4-0s of 1885, but had a Belpaire firebox. It had 17in x 24in cylinders, 160psi boiler pressure, 6ft 1in driving wheels and weighed 39¼ tons. It was built to haul Woodford–Stratford through trains, and was the premier engine of this railway, and the later SMJctR. It is being turned at Stratford, wearing its original dark blue livery; other engines wore crimson lake. It became LMS No. 290, but was withdrawn in 1924.

Caledonian Railway

Although not the largest railway in Scotland, to all intents and purposes, with the travelling public, the CR stood at the forefront of railway operations north of the border. Much of this esteemed reputation emanated from the dynamism with which the CR ran its express trains. Unlike its senior rival, the NBR, not only did CR engines haul the Anglo-Scottish expresses on their own metals, but they regularly gave the best performance over the whole West Coast route. This high standard of running was repeated, with equal zest, on internal Scottish services. The supreme performance, and quality of service, was due to the fierce pride, and 'family' loyalty, that permeated the employees, from the boardroom to the workers at all levels. This, and the rivalry with the NBR and G&SWR, ensured that the CR was second to nobody with its train services, either in Scotland, or elsewhere in Britain for that matter.

The CR was empowered by an Act of Parliament, in 1845, to build a railway from Carlisle to Carstairs, with lines running from there to Glasgow, Edinburgh and the Scottish Central Railway, to Stirling. The lines were engineered by none other than Joseph Locke, and all were completed by 1848, thus giving the first through route from London to Scotland.

During the next two decades, the CR absorbed many smaller railways and built its own lines to reach Aberdeen in the north, Oban in the north west, Wemyss Bay along the River Clyde, and Ardrossan on the west coast. There was also much development around Glasgow, including the new Central station. Two absorbed railways are of interest; the Glasgow & Garnkirk Railway, opened in 1831, adding to the CR ancestry, and the Callander & Oban Railway, opened in 1880, contributing to the romance of the CR. This latter line ran through the desolate country one associates with Highland clans and Bonnie Prince Charlie; in fact, the branch to Ballachulish ran near to the bottom of Glencoe.

As has been suggested, the CR gained considerable prestige through the running of its trains, and obviously this was dependent on the engines available. Robert Sinclair was the first Locomotive Superintendent, based at the Greenock Works. However, most engines at that time were designed by Allen, at Crewe, being of the 2-2-2 type, and in 1856 Sinclair moved to the ECR. Benjamin Connor took over, and he supervised the moving of the works to St Rollox in 1859. Connor designed many 2-4-0s, and his 8ft 2in 'single', was rated second only to Stirling's on the GNR. He began the tradition of high quality CR engines, and was succeeded by George Brittain in 1879. Brittain continued Connor's work, building on proven designs.

In 1882 Dugald Drummond moved across from the NBR, and transformed the locomotive stock in just eight years. His best designs were the inside cylinder 4-4-0s, which set new standards of Scottish locomotive performance. Drummond left for Australia, and was replaced by Hugh Smellie, from the rival G&SWR; there was no doubt now, as to which was the premier railway in Scotland. He died in the year of appointment, to be succeeded by Hugh Lambie, who followed a similar locomotive building policy to Drummond, until he too died, in 1895.

It was during the 19 years with J. F. McIntosh in charge of design, that the CR produced possibly the best contemporary locomotives in Britain. The four classes of 'Dunalastair' 4-4-0s had a superb reputation, and the 49 and 'Cardean' classes of express 4-6-0s set standards of running unequalled in Britain. The mighty *Cardean* itself took "The Corridor" in both directions, between Glasgow and Carlisle, daily for the first ten years of its life. McIntosh's mixed traffic 4-6-0s and goods engines were also outstanding performers. Sadly, CR designs seemed to stagnate during the final years with W. Pickersgill, from the GNSR, in charge of locomotive matters. This might have accounted for the early demise of many CR engines in the post-1923 LMS company.

If it was the sight of the expresses, dashingly hauled by the engines of Drummond and McIntosh which caught the public's imagination, much of the CR consisted of single track branches. Though lacking the glamour of the main lines, these were run with the same pride, and passengers and goods were well cared for. As with many railways, this was the 'bread and butter' of the business, and the keen rivalry, especially with the NBR, ensured high standards.

Alongside its railway activities, the CR had an extensive fleet of steamships, based on the Clyde. These offered both pleasure and service travel, and by 1900 were covering more than half a million miles annually. There was also docks at Leith and Grangemouth on the Forth, mainly used for coal traffic.

If much ink has been spilt on this brief history, for so few pictures, this is due to the deserving nature of the CR. By 1913 it was the seventh largest railway in Britain, by route mileage, and paid steady dividends. Its passenger, and especially express services, like the locomotives, were up with the best at the time, and far and away above those of the rival NBR. Yet after Grouping, the CR lost much of its identity, especially regarding locomotive matters. For a company, whose blue engines came to personify speed and reliability, this was something of an undeserved end.

J. F. McIntosh's 766 'Dunalastair II' class 4-4-0 No. 776, built in 1897 for the Caledonian Railway, is at Aberdeen during its early days. On the Glasgow–Aberdeen service these powerful engines could take twice the load of the 1895 'race' trains, at the same speeds. They were also regular engines on "The Corridor", from Carlisle to Glasgow, with a 2hr 15mins schedule, and were capable of 80mph. The photographer has described these as the "Breadalbane" class, and they had 19in x 26in cylinders, 175psi boiler pressure, 6ft 6in driving wheels, 17,900lbs T.E. and weighed 52 tons 16 cwt, with 32 tons for adhesion. Five engines of this design were ordered by the Belgian Railways.

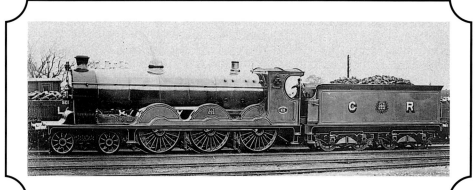

When J. F. McIntosh was the Locomotive Superintendent, the CR had a stud of passenger engines the equal of any in Britain. His 49 class, introduced in 1903, were the most powerful passenger engines in Britain. They had 21in x 26in cylinders, 200psi boiler pressure, 6ft 6in driving wheels, 25,000lbs T.E. and weighed 73 tons. The two engines were designed to haul the 2pm "Corridor", London–Glasgow express, which was often loaded to 400 tons. No. 49 is seen here when new, making an impressive sight with its 5 ton coal capacity tender and modern looks.

No. 574 arrives at the Wemyss Bay terminus, with a train carrying some enthusiastic passengers. CR boats departed from here for the island of Bute, and still do today, and it was a popular escape for Glaswegians. Another engine awaits its next duty beside the signal box.

Glasgow & South Western Railway

The constituent companies of the G&SWR were opened before both the rival CR and NBR companies had obtained their respective Acts of Parliament, but it became hemmed in the south west corner of Scotland. Indeed, its territory was subject to an occasional incursion by the hostile CR, especially around Glasgow and the Clyde coast. It is this rivalry that stands out in the history of both these railways, often the partisanship among patrons being as fierce and loyal as that of the employees. Despite being outgrown by the two senior Scottish railways, the G&SWR never gave ground, or concessions, throughout its existence.

The Glasgow, Paisley, Kilmarnock & Ayr Railway was opened by 1840, connecting with the Glasgow, Dumfries & Carlisle Railway shortly afterwards. Following failed overtures to the LNWR and CR, these two amalgamated to form the G&SWR in 1850. The CR took the Anglo-Scottish traffic, so the G&SWR concentrated on developing routes to Ayr and Ardrossan. In 1862 the Portpatrick & Wigtownshire Railway opened, connecting with the G&SWR at Castle Douglas, and later opening the port of Stranraer as the shortest point of departure for Ireland. This route was further enhanced when the Ulster-bound Royal Mails were diverted that way. Stranraer was also reached by the Ayrshire & Wigtownshire Railway via Girvan, absorbed in 1891, thus opening a direct route from Glasgow. The PWR was jointly owned with the MR, LNWR and CR and the G&SWR worked it on a three year rota with the CR.

1876 was a memorable year, as the MR opened its Settle and Carlisle route, thus beginning through Anglo-Scottish services using the G&SWR north of the border, and the imposing St Enoch station was opened in Glasgow. The G&SWR was now in a position to challenge the CR on prestige services, especially as the two companies had recently built a shorter, joint route from Glasgow to Kilmarnock. Nevertheless, it was in and around Glasgow, and on the Clyde coast services, that rivalry was still at its fiercest, though the 1870s had seen the G&SWR status rise considerably.

In the earlier years, the G&SWR engines did not give second best to the CR, and it was probably the spirited challenge from the G&SWR, when the CR was in the ascendancy, that drove the latter to keep producing ever-more powerful designs. None other than the latterly 'great' Patrick Stirling was the first Locomotive Superintendent, and in 1856 he moved the works to Kilmarnock. He designed some useful 2-2-2s for passenger services, and 0-4-2s for goods trains. It must be remembered that the G&SWR was not a major through railway when he left for the GNR in 1866. He was succeeded by his brother James, who carried on the family tradition of domeless boilers. James designed some fast 4-4-0s, which performed well on both the Stranraer, and new Anglo-Scottish, services before departing for the SER in 1878. Hugh Smellie arrived from the Maryport & Carlisle Railway and, in many respects, emulated the Stirlings. He left for the rival CR in 1890, but died after a few months in office.

As with the CR, the heavier Anglo-Scottish expresses on the G&SWR needed more powerful engines by this century. J. Manson responded by designing the 381 class, built at the newly formed North British Locomotive Co. in 1903. These had 20in x 26in cylinders, 180psi boiler pressure, 6ft 6in driving wheels, 20,320lbs T.E. and weighed 67 tons. They were often compared unfavourably with the CR 49 class, but due to weight restrictions on the G&SWR route, these engines were not built as solidly as desired. This hampered their uphill running, but they regularly ran to over 80mph on favourable stretches. This picture of No. 384 was taken at NBL when it was new. All ten were withdrawn between 1927 and 1933.

At that point in time the G&SWR had one of the best studs of locomotives in Britain; it was no fault of James Manson, from the GNSR, that this position changed slightly. His 4-4-0s were fine engines, though over-shadowed by the various 'Dunalastairs', of the CR, and he matched the CR 4-6-0s with his own designs. But the G&SWR was not a big company, and did not have the need for a large stock of engines; its longest line was less than 120 miles. In 1912 Peter Drummond arrived from the HR. He was not as talented as his famous brother and his 'scrap and build' policy weakened the locomotive stock. Finally, Robert Whitelegg, formerly of the LTSR, took over in 1918.

He improved many of Manson's designs, and built some powerful tank engines, before the Grouping in 1923.

Though latterly over-shadowed by the CR, the G&SWR matched it in many respects. It also had a small fleet of ships operating on the Clyde, and many were the races between the rival crews, often with the CR being left behind. Also, its shareholders often received a better dividend than did those investing in the CR. It was mainly the rivalry and enthusiasm of the two sets of employees that kept the standards of operation so high on both railways, for the benefit of all concerned, staff, passengers and investors alike.

J. Stirling's 208 class was very similar to his brother's 0-4-2s for the GNR. Sixty were built by Neilson and Dübs between 1873 and 1878, for mixed traffic duties. They had 18in x 26in cylinders, 140psi boiler pressure and 5ft 7½in driving wheels. No. 211, built in 1873 and scrapped in 1923, is standing at Glasgow St Enoch. Some of these were rebuilt with superheaters and domed boilers, and four survived until 1930–1. The Stirling family design traits are clearly seen here.

Manson's 326 class 0-4-4T, was a typical passenger tank of the late Victorian era. Like many of their contemporaries in England, these found employment on suburban services, mostly around Glasgow. They had 17½in x 24in cylinders, 5ft 2in driving wheels and weighed 51 tons, and all, except No. 328, were rebuilt. This engine is seen on a Glasgow local train. It was scrapped in 1931.

Highland Railway

For those who were railway 'romantics' the HR had everything; graceful bridges, sweeping curves, tight cuttings and distinguished viaducts; all running through some of the wildest and most rugged countryside in Britain. Mountains peered down over the line, rivers sent it this way and that, while the lochs serenely kept their distance from the invading 'iron road'. If a crow decided to fly from Stanley Junction, near Perth, where the HR joined the CR, to Thurso in the far north, it would travel about 135 miles. However, if it made the mistake of following the HR line for a change, the poor bird would be less in the mood for a bit of fun on arrival, having had to fly twice the distance. Such was the difficult terrain the HR had to plod through.

At the turn of the century the HR owned just over 500 route miles, much of it single track and, as such, it was in the third rank of pre-Grouping companies. Yet, in terms of traffic carried, locomotives per route mile, coaches and wagons owned, it was right down at the bottom, along with the minor railways. Glorious though the scenery alongside much of the HR might have been, the land was sparsely populated, and the railway difficult and expensive to work. Thus, many of its services were unremunerative, and one wonders just how it managed to keep going.

Keep going, though, it did. The HR was formed in 1865 by an amalgamation of the Inverness & Aberdeen Junction Railway and the Inverness & Perth Junction Railway. These, in their turn, had previously absorbed smaller railways and, altogether, nine companies were eventually constituted into the HR,

including the Duke of Sutherland's own private railway, which still forms part of the main line to Thurso. The line from Perth, which offered valuable connections to the south, ran to Inverness, the hub of the system. From there, lines meandered north to Wick and Thurso, opened in 1874, west to Strome Ferry, opened in 1870, and finally, Kyle of Lochalsh, in 1897. East from Inverness, a line joined the GNSR, at Keith, to give a through route to Aberdeen; this being the oldest part of the system. No matter which route one considers though, each was the same; long distances, remote villages and little intermediate traffic.

Locomotive needs were quite unlike those of other railways, there was no chance of sustained high-speed running here. Tight curves and steep hills predominated, and although loads were often light, they could become very heavy during the shooting season. The first Locomotive Superintendent was William Stroudley, from 1866. He did not design much in his three years before moving on to the LBSCR, but he rationalised the diverse locomotive stock inherited from the smaller companies, and began engine building at the Lochgorm Works, in Inverness. David Jones took over for the next 27 years, and designed many excellent 4-4-0s, including the 'Duke' class, the most powerful engines in Britain when introduced. The development of that design culminated in the 'Loch' class, pictured here; fine passenger engines, the equal of any in the country. But Jones is perhaps best known for building the first 4-6-0s in Britain, the famous 'Jones goods'. These were a fine epitaph, as they were his last design.

D. Jones last design of passenger 4-4-0 for the Highland Railway was the 119, or 'Loch', class of 1896. These had 19in x 24in cylinders, 175psi boiler pressure, 6ft 3in driving wheels, 15,600lbs T.E. and weighed 49 tons. No. 126 Loch Tummel is standing in front of No. 120 of the same class. Fifteen were built in 1896, followed by three more in 1917, and they worked the London–Inverness expresses from Perth, until the 1930s. Loch Tummel was withdrawn in 1938, but two survived until 1950.

Peter Drummond succeeded Jones, building the fine 'Castle' class 4-6-0, probably a development of Jones own design for a passenger version of his 'goods'. Drummond was not in the same class as his famous brother Dugald, nor Jones, and his other designs were merely adequate. F. G. Smith succeeded Drummond, when he left for the G&SWR in 1911, and he was noted for building the excellent 'River' class 4-6-0s. These were unacceptable to the Civil Engineer, as being too heavy, and had to be sold to the CR. C. Cumming and D. C. Urie, the son of R. Urie of the LSWR, were the final two in charge of locomotive design.

The HR thus trod an uneasy path, both financially and operationally. Yet, for all its problems, the HR was a valuable, if not vital, link for those communities it served. In many respects this can be the only reason for building some of the lines, and, unlike many other railways, the HR did not abandon those isolated places when traffic fell below expectations, or the fierce winter set in. It took the politicians behind BR to do that.

Great Western Railway

Few people with an interest in railways remain either impartial, or apathetic, where the GWR is concerned. This, no doubt, is due to its unique position among the highly diversified bunch of railways that operated in Britain before 1923. It distanced itself from the other railways being built, or planned in the 1830s, by using a gauge of 7ft 0¼in. Right from the outset, as suggested by the early adoption of such a grandiose title, the GWR intended to have a sphere of operation which precluded any of the 'standard gauge' brigade.

Alone among the senior pre-Grouping companies, the GWR survived, with important additions, until nationalisation in 1948. Yet in the 115 years since the first prospectus for the Bristol & London Railway was issued, a major character transformation had taken place. With Isambard Kingdom Brunel in charge of the route planning, and Daniel Gooch controlling locomotive and stock designs, the GWR sallied forth in a maverick fashion. Each magnificent success, like the excellent London–Bristol route, seemed to be followed by an equally significant disaster, such as Brunel's ill-fated atmospheric experiment on the South Devon Railway. Gooch produced the fastest engines in the world, only for the Gauges Commission to rule against further expansion of Brunel's beloved 'broad gauge'. By 1910 the old broad gauge had long been swept away, and the GWR was proceeding with a standardisation plan for locomotives, stock and operating mechanisms, undreamed of elsewhere in Britain.

It was during those idiosyncratic, pioneering days that the GWR character and ambitions were formed. From the initial London–Bristol trunk, opened throughout in 1841, broad gauge lines pushed onward to Wolverhampton, South Wales via Gloucester and into the South West, eventually reaching Penzance and Weymouth. However, at Gloucester, where connections were made with the BGR, and northwards from Oxford, the first problems were encountered with the rival 'standard gauge'. The line from Oxford to Wolverhampton, via Birmingham, was built for mixed gauge use, and this was extended southwards to Basingstoke. North of Wolverhampton the GWR eventually reached Birkenhead, but these lines were built to standard gauge only, and by 1861 mixed gauge lines entered Paddington, offering through standard gauge running from London to Hereford and Birkenhead. The death knell for the broad gauge began to ring loud and clear.

Upon the death of Brunel, shortly after the opening of his noble Royal Albert Bridge over the River Tamar in 1859, the GWR seemed to regress. Despite the gradual change-over to mixed and standard gauge lines, and the steady absorption of allied railways in Wales and the South West, standards of service began to deteriorate. Whereas, in the earlier days, the broad gauge expresses were both fast and punctual, the reverse was becoming more commonplace. With the eventual, and inevitable, demise of the broad gauge, there was a reluctance to invest in new locomotives and coaches, with the result that during a period of rapid improvements elsewhere, the old GWR was, at best, standing still. Physical appearances were kept up, but this could not hide the reality of decline.

Furthermore, as railways were being pushed into all parts of the kingdom, requiring new main lines, the GWR was still centred on its London–Bristol trunk. The GWR initials became popularly known as the 'Great Way Round', an unkind, but nevertheless true, witticism. It was during Daniel Gooch's time as Chairman, that plans to improve the system were laid. After lengthy struggles against flooding, the Severn Tunnel was opened in 1886, shortening the route to South Wales. Gooch himself was the first person through the tunnel, having to crawl through a small hole during a visit, no doubt bringing back memories of his friend Brunel.

Apart from public jibes about 'Great Way Round', there were all manner of problems associated with long routes. On lines competing with other railways, like the London–Birmingham, the opposition ran the quicker times, and on routes without competition, such as London–South Wales, costs were high, due to the mileage. In 1903 the South Wales line was shortened still further with the opening of the Badminton cut-off, and compared to 20 years before, journey times were reduced by a third. Three years later, journey times to the West of England were reduced significantly, with the opening of the necessary sections to allow running via Westbury. This effectively ended serious LSWR competition on the London–Exeter route. In 1908 the Birmingham–Cheltenham line was completed, enabling the GWR to compete against the MR for Midlands–South Wales/Bristol traffic. Finally, in 1910, the Bicester cut off, part of which was shared with the GCR, was finished. The GWR could now also run London–Birmingham trains in two hours, competing directly with the LNWR. These new routes offered the opportunity for much faster trains, providing the locomotives were available. Fortunately, the GWR was served excellently in that direction.

Daniel Gooch became the first Locomotive Superintendent in 1837, and was as much a pioneer in his own field, as was Brunel in his several fields. He bought the first engines from northern locomotive builders, but these proved to be very unsatisfactory and, after establishing the new works at Swindon, the first engines were built there in 1846. Gooch is perhaps best remembered for his 'Firefly' class, and especially the majestic 4-2-2 engines, which gleamed at the head of broad gauge expresses.

Gooch retired in 1864 and was replaced by Joseph Armstrong from the works at Wolverhampton. Armstrong's brother George, took over his position there, and retained a fair amount of autonomy, until 1896. It was left to Armstrong to begin the transition from 'broad' to 'standard' gauge. Having been brought up in a northern engineering background, this task was more than adequately performed, and the basis for future designs were laid without losing the best of the broad gauge traditions of speed and reliability.

In 1877 Armstrong was succeeded by William Dean. Here was another of those formidable Victorian autocrats who ranked alongside his contemporaries Webb, Drummond and P. Stirling. The term 'great' can be used to describe any of those engineers, and it was not long before Dean was showing his prowess. He ensured that the old broad gauge engines were maintained to a highly respectable degree, until the end in 1892, while he instigated the design of a continuously improving stock of standard gauge engines. Some of these are featured in the following pages and, apart from the obvious family resemblance, most were highly successful, providing the ideal springboard from which his successor, in 1902, George Jackson Churchward, could take the locomotive world by storm. Little needs to be said here about how Churchward standardised his designs to a remarkable degree, being clearly right at the forefront of British locomotive practice until he retired in 1922, and layed the traditions followed faithfully by his successors, until Nationalisation.

The GWR did not restrict its activities solely to railways either. It eventually had more ports than any other railway, with steamers going to the Channel Islands, Scilly Isles and Ireland. Omnibus services appeared fairly extensively, especially in the West Country and, albeit after Grouping, the pioneering Brunel/Gooch spirit rose again with the introduction of internal air services. No doubt those pioneers would have been impressed with that.

The GWR had firmly established itself in the 'first division' of pre-Grouping railways in Edwardian Britain. In most respects it was second only to the LNWR, like turnover, number of engines and so forth, but it had the longest route mileage by nearly 800 miles. Dividends, which had slumped to $1\frac{3}{8}\%$ in 1868, were consistently above 4% from then on, and in 1910 the GWR paid the third highest dividend of any major railway. The disasters had also been well and truly eliminated from GWR activities, but the price for this was the lack of the flamboyant brilliance of the Brunel/Gooch era. Oh yes, there was the dash of the "Ocean Mail" specials, and the non-stop "Cornish Riviera Limited" but, excellent though they were, the sight of a Churchward engine in full cry never quite excited in the way that a Gooch 'single', or Gresley Pacific, did.

Then again, none of the 'first division' railways of LNWR, MR, NER and GWR, displayed a quixotic character, but all were quietly efficient. This was how they rose to their pre-eminent position among Britain's railways. Thanks initially to Gooch, when Chairman, and later standardisation policies, the 'Great Way Round' was transformed into 'God's Wonderful Railway', full of its unique character, while reflecting the area it served more so than any other railway. It was just regrettable that the 'golden years' of Gooch/Brunel had to pass, before the GWR truly realised its potential.

Arguably the most successful of all pre-Grouping passenger engines, was Churchward's 'Star' class 4-6-0, built between 1906 and 1923, for the Great Western Railway, which formed the basis of the later 'Castles' and 'Kings'. With four 15in x 26in cylinders, 225psi boiler pressure, 6ft 8½in driving wheels, 27,800lbs T.E. and weighing 76 tons, with 56 tons for adhesion, they were certainly the most powerful express passenger engines of their day. No. 4007 Rising Star, *built in 1907, is ready for its next duty, at Exeter St Davids. It was later renamed* Swallowfield Park, *and passed onto BR. Withdrawal of the class began in 1932, but was not completed until 1957.*

'Star' class No. 4018 Knight of the Grand Cross, *built in 1908, is at Plymouth Millbay having been re-coaled and made ready for its next duty. Earlier, it had brought the non-stop "Cornish Riviera Limited" from Paddington, scheduled to run the 226 miles in 247 minutes, the longest non-stop run in the world at the time. These magnificent engines spent their whole lives on main line passenger duties, and did not suffer the indignities heaped on many engines, when superseded by more modern designs. They remain the epitome of Edwardian steam engines.*

G. J. Churchward's first 'Saint' class, No. 100 William Dean, *built in 1902, stands at Taunton in 1903, before being rebuilt with a tapered boiler, later that year. It was originally built while Dean was still in charge at Swindon, but it bears all the hallmarks of what became the renowned Churchward style. Once Dean had retired the engine was named Dean, but this was changed soon afterwards. This had 18½in x 30in cylinders, 200psi (later 225psi) boiler pressure, 6ft 8½in driving wheels, 24,395lbs T.E. and weighed 72 tons. Although many 'Saints' passed onto BR, this historically important engine was scrapped in 1932.*

An unidentified 'Saint', with a typical GWR 'period' train, heads towards Exeter, alongside the sea wall at Dawlish. The uniformity of the coaches can be compared favourably with those of other railways featured in this book. This location remains one of the finest places to watch trains, even today.

No. 2928 Saint Sebastian, *built in 1907, stands behind Exeter St Davids station, before rebuilding, and the removal of the station's overall roof. There were eventually 77 'Saints' and, along with the 4-cylinder 'Stars', they bore the brunt of GWR express passenger services for over 20 years. Forty-seven 'Saints' passed onto BR, still working passenger trains.*

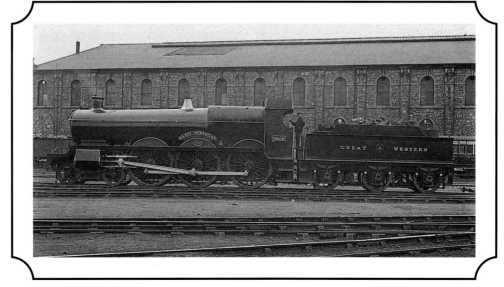

A drab 'official' picture of a very interesting engine. Du Bousquet de Glehn 4-cylinder compound, No. 102 La France, *was built in 1903 by the Société Alsacienne de Constructions Mecaniques, in France, and imported for comparative purposes. Compounding was not adopted by Churchward, but many other features were. Dimensions were 13³/₈in x 25 ³/₁₆in H.P. cylinders, 22¹/₁₆in x 25³/₁₆ in L.P. cylinders, 227psi boiler pressure, 29¹/₂ sq ft grate, 6ft 8¹/₂in driving wheels and 65 tons weight. On its inaugural Paddington–Exeter run,* La France *maintained 85mph on dead level track, with a full load. This engine survived until 1926, often to be seen on Oxford–Birmingham services.*

Following the delivery of La France, *Churchward introduced the 14 engines of the 172 class Atlantics, in 1904. They had 18in x 30in cylinders, 6ft 8¹/₂in driving wheels, 225psi boiler pressure, 27 sq ft grate, 23,000lbs T.E. and weighed 70¹/₂ tons, 39 tons for adhesion. No. 180, seen here at Plymouth Laira, was named* Coeur de Lion, *and was converted to a 'Saint' class 4-6-0 in 1912.*

W. Dean turned to 4-4-0s for his final passenger designs. His 'Badminton' class of 1897 were the first GWR engines to use a Belpaire firebox, and had 18in x 26in cylinders, 6ft 8in driving wheels and 180psi boiler pressure. No. 3296 Cambria, *seen here alongside some interesting adverts at Newport, began life on express trains. Although quickly displaced by the 'Saint' class on such services, the majority of 'Badmintons' survived into the early 1930s, on secondary duties.*

'Duke' class No. 3316 Isle of Guernsey, *built in 1899, awaits its next duty, at Westbourne Park. The prominent, highly polished dome was to disappear on later deigns. The 'Dukes' originally had 18in x 26in cylinders, 160psi boiler pressure, 5ft 8in driving wheels, 16,848lbs T.E. and weighed 46 tons, with 28$\frac{1}{2}$ tons for adhesion.*

The Penzance portion of the 10.50am ex-Paddington, the "Cornish Riviera Limited", leaves Truro behind 'Camel' class 4-4-0 No. 3463 Vancouver, *built in 1904. This class, built from 1898, was used on secondary express trains, such as those in Cornwall, and had 18in x 26in cylinders, 200psi boiler pressure, 5ft 8in driving wheels, 21,060lbs T.E. and weighed 52 tons. They varied widely in terms of firebox, boiler, frames and domes, though this did not prevent many passing onto BR, No. 3463 not being scrapped until 1949, as No. 3401. These later became known as the 'Bulldog' class.*

Dean's 'Atbara' class was introduced in 1900, and they proved to be excellent express passenger engines. They had 18in x 26in cylinders, 195psi boiler pressure, 6ft 8$\frac{1}{2}$in driving wheels, 17,345lbs T.E. and weighed 51 tons 12 cwt. No. 3373 Atbara *later No. 4120, was built in 1900, receives attention at Westbourne Park shed. All the 'Atbara's' were withdrawn by 1931.*

'Atbara' class No. 3390 Terrible, *later No. 4136, built in 1900, shows off its massive build at Plymouth Millbay. Though quickly displaced off the fastest expresses by the 'Saints' and 'Stars', 'Atbaras' like the other 4-4-0s, spent many years on secondary expresses, such as the South Wales/Bristol–Birmingham services, until withdrawals began in the late 1920s.*

'Atbara' class No. 3376 Herschel, *built in 1900, and Churchward's 'City' class No. 3433* City of Bath, *later No. 3710, built in 1903, stand amidst the light rays streaming through the roof at Paddington. The 'Cities' had 18in x 26in cylinders, 200psi boiler pressure, 6ft 8½in driving wheels, 18,000lbs T.E. and weighed 55½ tons. City of Bath covered itself, and the GWR, in glory in 1903, by hauling the Royal Train non-stop from Paddington–Plymouth in 233min. 35sec. at an average speed of 63–64mph, symbolising the arrival of the new, Edwardian era. It was superheated in 1918, but was withdrawn as early as 1929.*

Churchward's 'City' class combined Victorian design principles, such as outside frames, with the very latest in locomotive design, like the Belpaire firebox and tapered boiler. No. 3441 City of Winchester, *later No. 3718, had a short life: built in 1903, superheated in 1911 and scrapped in 1927. This was not due to any deficiency with the class, rather the excellence of other Swindon designs. It is likely that these popular engines would have enjoyed much longer lives on any of the other 'Big Four' railways.*

Widely regarded as the least successful of all Churchward's standard classes, the 'Counties' differed from the earlier 4-4-0s in having outside cylinders. They were intended to work passenger trains on routes where the 4-6-0s were not permitted. Having 18in x 30in cylinders, 200psi boiler pressure, 6ft 8½in driving wheels, 20,530lbs T.E. and weighing 55 tons 6 cwt, with 38 tons for adhesion, they were fast and powerful engines. However, their rough riding did not encourage drivers to run fast, and they were quickly relegated to cross-country services. Forty engines were built between 1904 and 1912, and No. 3818 County of Radnor, *built in 1906, is ready for the road, at Plymouth Laira. The 'Counties' were withdrawn 1930–3.*

Another fine picture of a GWR 4-4-0, at Plymouth Millbay; this time 'Flower' class No. 4106 Campanula, built in 1908. These had 18in x 26in cylinders, 195psi boiler pressure, 6ft 8½in driving wheels, 17,345lbs T.E. and weighed 53 tons 6 cwt. In many respects these were a development of the 'Cities', and proved to be the final GWR inside cylinder 4-4-0, with double frames. Starting life on express duties, these were, like the other 4-4-0s, soon demoted to secondary duties, and all 20 were scrapped 1927–31. It is sad to recall the rapid demise of the GWR 4-4-0s, from the late 1920s. These fine engines had many useful years work in them when withdrawn, but had been supplanted by the excellent range of engines emerging from Swindon at that time.

A faded, but interesting picture of 'Queen' class 2-2-2 No. 1129, built in 1875. These had 18in x 24in cylinders, 140psi boiler pressure, 7ft driving wheels, 11,016lbs T.E. and weighed 33½ tons, with 14 tons for adhesion. Despite their modest size, they hauled the fastest 'narrow gauge' expresses until the end of the last century. No. 1129 is seen at Westbourne Park and has been rebuilt with a domeless boiler and Belpaire firebox, and features the GWR crest on its splasher.

The crew of 'Queen' class No. 1133, built in 1875 and seen in original condition, are proud to pose with their immaculate engine, while at Westbourne Park. In their latter years, the 'Queens' worked the Oxford–Worcester–Wolverhampton route, often taking trains of up to 300 tons. On these duties they outlived the larger 4-2-2s, but as with 'singles' elsewhere, once displaced from express duties, suitable work was difficult to find, and many engines were withdrawn before their time.

W. Dean's 'Queen' class No. 1125, built in 1875, passes Handsworth (Birmingham) at high speed, with the 2.10pm express from Paddington. The uniform nature of these coaches clearly enhance the visual aspect of the train, a common feature of the GWR at this time. The lady companion, standing beside the telegraph pole, is of interest, as she did not become the photographer's wife! No. 1125 was withdrawn in 1906.

This scene at Westbourne Park features Dean's 157, or 'Cobham' class 2-2-2 No. 160, built in 1879, and rebuilt with a Belpaire firebox, but retaining the polished dome. With 18in x 24in cylinders, 140psi boiler pressure, 7ft driving wheels, 11,000lbs T.E. and weighing 36 tons, the 'Cobhams' remained on express services into this century. No. 165 of this class was the last GWR 'single' to be withdrawn, in 1914; No. 160 suffered this fate in 1905.

The 30 engines of Dean's 3000 class, built in 1891/2, had short, but interesting lives. They were originally built as 2-2-2s, eight of which were originally broad gauge engines. The whole class were rebuilt as 4-2-2s following the 1894 Box Tunnel derailment, and some also received a Belpaire firebox and domeless boiler. They had 20in x 24in cylinders, 160psi boiler pressure, 7ft 8in driving wheels, 12,800lbs T.E. and weighed 49 tons. No. 3027 Worcester *took its name from 'Cobham' class No. 158 in 1895, and is seen in rebuilt form at Taunton, with a West of England train.*

Dean's 2201 class, designed for secondary passenger duties, was one of the 'lesser lights' alongside his 'singles' and 4-4-0s. The crew of No. 2205, built in 1881, are still proud enough to be photographed with their engine. With 17in x 24in cylinders, 140psi boiler pressure, 6ft 6in driving wheels, 10,298lbs T.E. and weighing 32 tons 8 cwt, they were never very powerful engines, but were still used to pilot cross-country expresses until the last was withdrawn in 1913. Ten of these engines were built in 1882, with domeless boilers.

An unidentified Dean 4-2-2 passing a typical GWR water tower, with the "Cornishman", at high speed. This lovely photograph shows a typical 'period' GWR express, with a uniform coaching set, hauled by an impeccably turned out 'single', running to some of the fastest schedules in the country.

Armstrong's 388 class, 'old standard goods' 0-6-0s eventually numbered 310 engines, and worked throughout the GWR standard gauge system. They had 17in x 24in cylinders, 140psi boiler pressure, 5ft wheels, weighed 30 tons and were ideal goods engines, although it was not unknown for them to reach 60mph on main line passenger duties, in an emergency. No. 799, built in 1873, looks healthy enough, at Westbourne Park. It was withdrawn in 1918, but some survived into the 1930s.

Dean's 'Standard goods', built from 1883 until 1898, eventually numbered 240 engines, some surviving for over 70 years. These were the first GWR engines to have inside frames and although differing in details, had 17$\frac{1}{2}$in x 24in cylinders, 180psi boiler pressure, 5 ft 2in wheels, 18,140lbs T.E. and weighed 36$\frac{3}{4}$ tons. Most of these 0-6-0s spent their lives on goods and branch lines themselves. No. 2569, built in 1898, was one of over 50 which passed onto BR, although it was withdrawn in 1948. It is seen here at Westbourne Park, alongside 'single' No. 3003, and is ready for its duties.

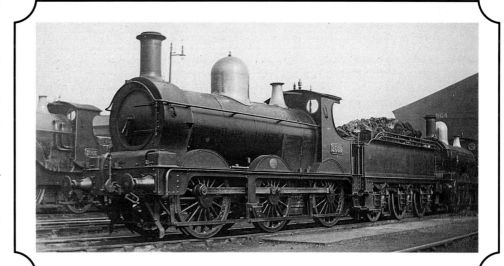

Churchward's 3150 class, built 1906–8, was the first development of his '31xx' class of Prairie tanks. No. 3188, built in 1907, pictured behind Exeter St Davids, is a splendid example of this class when new. They had 18$\frac{1}{2}$ x 30in cylinders, 200psi boiler pressure, 5ft 8in driving wheels, 25,670lbs T. E. and weighed 82 tons, with 58 tons for adhesion. Their duties were both numerous, and wide ranging, from heavy mineral trains in South Wales, to passenger trains and Severn Tunnel banking duties. The last of these 41 genuine 'all rounders' was withdrawn in 1958.

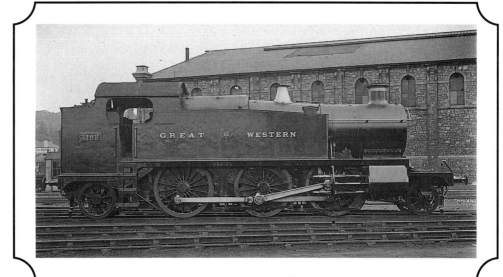

'Light Prairie' tank No. 2169, built at Wolverhampton in 1907, poses with its crew at Plymouth Millbay, when new. This was a member of the 4500 class of 1906, which was itself a development of the 4400 class of two years earlier. They had 17in x 24in cylinders, 200psi boiler pressure, 4ft 7½in driving wheels, 21,250lbs T.E. and weighed 57 tons. The 175 engines in this class worked the lighter branches throughout the GWR system, and were joined by up-dated versions, designed by Collett, in the late 1920s.

Dean's 3600 class 'double-ender' 2-4-2T of 1900-3, was influenced by Webb's similar designs for the LNWR. Using the 'Camel' class boiler etc. they had 17in x 24in cylinders, 200psi boiler pressure, 5ft 2in driving wheels, 18,000lbs T.E. and weighed 65 tons, with 35 tons for adhesion. No. 3607, built in 1900, was rebuilt and superheated, like others in the class, by Churchward. They were removed from their initial duties when the Prairies arrived, and worked their remaining time out, until withdrawn by the early 1930s, on lighter workings.

4-4-0T No. 1307, probably built in 1880, rests amidst a rural setting, at Truro. Unfortunately, details of this locomotive have proved to be elusive, but at the time the photograph was taken, c1900, it was used for working the Perranporth branch.

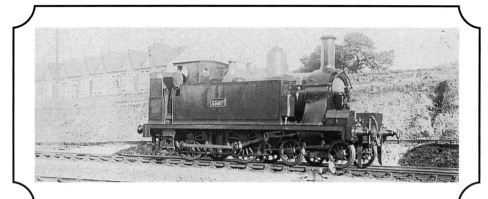

1501 class 0-6-0ST, known as 'Buffaloes', No. 1512, built at Wolverhampton in 1878, is dwarfed by its carriages as it waits to leave Bassaleg with a Newport train. They had 17in x 24in cylinders, 140psi boiler pressure, 4ft 7½in wheels, 15,935lbs T.E. and weighed 39 tons 8 cwt, and were used on a wide variety of light duties. Initially built without cabs, they received these before 1900, and were all later rebuilt as pannier tanks. They were all scrapped before 1948.

Looking through the GWR photographs in this collection, so many seem to be representative of the company: the 4-6-0s, Prairie tanks, Dean's goods, and now this Armstrong designed 0-4-2T. With 16in x 24in cylinders, 140psi boiler pressure, 5ft driving wheels, weighing 36¾ tons and with 26 tons for adhesion, these, and their much later developments, worked small branches right until the end of steam on the former GWR lines. No. 845, built at Wolverhampton in 1874, rests at Newport alongside some period advertisements.

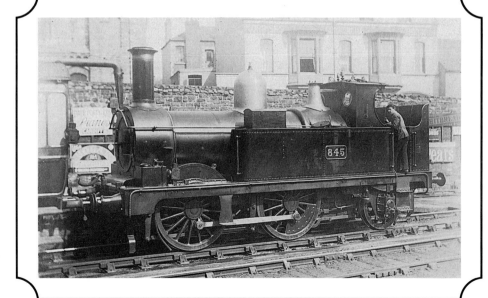

Midland & South Western Junction Railway

This relatively minor railway grew out of the grandiose plans, dating from the 1840s, for a Manchester–Southampton railway. Due to a variety of reasons, not least the fierce opposition from the GWR to a north/south route straight through its territory, it was not until 1873 that the Swindon, Marlborough & Andover Railway obtained an Act of Parliament which allowed building to commence. Even that took a long time to be organised and the line was not started until 1875, the Swindon–Marlborough section being opened in 1881, thence forward to Andover, using GWR metals from Marlborough to Savernake, two years later.

In 1881 the Swindon & Cheltenham Extension Railway began building north from Swindon and completed the route to Cirencester in 1883. This was worked by the SMAR from its opening and the two companies merged in 1884 to form the MSWJctR. This new venture was not exactly an outstanding success, and by the end of the year the company was in the hands of the Receiver.

Far from sounding the death-knell of the new company, that act led to both the numerous creditors, and the Receiver, deciding to press ahead with the building of the line to Cheltenham, an act seen as the only real means of survival. The new line was completed to Andoversford Junction, on the GWR Cheltenham–Banbury line, and running powers were obtained to join the Midland Railway at Cheltenham. Through services to Southampton from the Midlands began in 1892.

Until that time, the company was renowned for using borrowed coaches, unpunctuality, inefficiency and for its buildings and rolling stock having a generally unkempt appearance. All that began to change when the LSWR loaned Sam Fay to add his expertise, in 1892. A separate Marlborough–Grafton railway company was set up to build a line from Marlborough to Savernake, to overcome problems of using the GWR route between those places. This was absorbed by the MSWJctR in 1899, while in 1897 the company was finally removed from the receivership. New locomotives and coaches were eventually bought, and by the time Sam Fay returned to the LSWR in 1899, the MSWJctR, with 60 route miles, had finally established its existence, alongside the GWR.

To prepare for the expected boost to traffic, with the opening of the Cheltenham extension, the Midland & South Western Junction Railway ordered three of these 2-4-0s from Dübs in 1894. They had 17in x 24in cylinders, 150psi boiler pressure, 5ft 6in driving wheels, 13,399lbs T.E., weighed 35¾ tons and were used to haul the through Southampton boat trains, taking over at Cheltenham, until 1914. No. 12, seen here with its original stovepipe chimney, replaced in 1903, became GWR No. 1336 and was rebuilt at Swindon in 1924. It spent many years working in the Reading area and was the last to be withdrawn, in 1954, having run 506,867 miles, although all three passed onto BR. Of particular interest in this picture, is the grounded broad gauge coach body.

One could not expect such a small railway to flourish and grow, at least not one so dependent on the GWR, which regarded it as an interloper. True, the LSWR was happy for through traffic to and from Southampton to use the route, the more so as it cut right through the heart of GWR territory. However, traffic levels were always low, despite some improvement in through services in the Edwardian period. It was one of those lines that could only really survive thanks to the wasteful competitive spirit that existed between railway companies in those days. The MSWJctR was but a pawn in the far greater 'game' between the GWR and LSWR.

Nonetheless, 'every dog has its day', and the MSWJctR, after surviving happily enough as a poor relation alongside the other Swindon based railway, suddenly found itself thrust from deep in the railway 'chorus' to, if not the 'star of the show', at least a role with a recognisable character. World War One was the cause of this transformation, and with the Marlborough–Andover section passing through the army training grounds on Salisbury Plain, extra traffic was generated, often in batches far beyond the directors' wildest dreams. Fortunately for humanity, it did not last, and the company was finally absorbed by the GWR at the 1923 Grouping. Like so many little railways taken into the enhanced GWR, the MSWJctR lost its identity pretty rapidly, but once on the line, and away from the glare of the corporate publicity machine, and despite the GWR locomotives, the old character came to the fore again. Swindon only meant one thing to former MSWJctR employees, and it was nothing to do with that 'other' railway.

Taff Vale Railway

Of all the pre-Grouping railway companies, the TVR is probably one of the better known to the lay person with any knowledge of Economic History. It was authorised in 1836, and opened a line from Cardiff to Merthyr in 1841, extending out to Treherbert and Aberdare a few years later. This little 'valleys' railway eventually had 124 route miles and nearly 300 locomotives. Vast quantities of Welsh coal was transported to the docks at Cardiff and, as a result, the TVR paid, at one time, dividends approaching 20%, an enormous amount for the Victorian era. This was, surely, one of the jewels in the crowning glory of the British industrial revolution.

The TVR was in fierce competition with its many rivals, opening a line to Swansea in 1890 and, unsuccessfully, trying to reach Newport. Such was its profitability, that in 1894 the TVR introduced non-contributory pensions for employees with 25 years service, unheard of generosity for the time. However, following a ten day strike in 1900, over recognition of the Amalgamated Society of Railway Servants, during which the TVR used scab labour, the company claimed £23,000 compensation from the union: at that time the average manual worker received slightly less than £50 per year in wages. This was upheld a year later at the infamous 'Taff Vale Judgement', which effectively robbed unions and workers of the right to strike, until reversed several years later by the Liberal government. The recent Tory governments have done their best to reverse the position once again.

Despite its somewhat colourful history, the daily work of the TVR was lacking in glamour. Short distance passenger trains vied with an endless run of coal trains for track space, against the suitably drab back-cloth of industrial Wales. T. H. Hurry-Riches was the Locomotive Superintendent charged with providing the motive power for this diet of traffic, between 1873 and 1910. In the main, this warranted a large number of tank engines and a variety of 0-6-0 tender engines. Many were fine locomotives, and played their part in the profitability of the company by leading suitably lengthy lives; who could ask for more? Hurry-Riches went on to become the President of the Institute of Mechanical Engineers for 1906–7, an honour amply justified by his sturdy, reliable, no-nonsense designs.

As with the other 'Welsh valleys' railways, the TVR operations were run as a strictly 'no frills' affair. After the events of 1900, the TVR could not even boast of being a 'happy family', as could its rivals, but it retained the position of 'top dog' in the 'valleys'. There were other compensations as well. Shareholders of the GWR may well have basked in the reflected glory of that company's achievements, but those of the TVR had a far better financial return on their investment. On purely business grounds, which is an important yard-stick by which to judge a company, the TVR succeeded better than any other railway in Britain. However, for all its commercial success, the TVR is best remembered for the way it acted during a ten day period; history can be unforgiving at times.

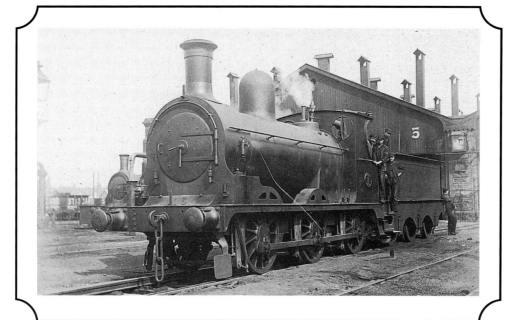

A posse of railway workers gather around Taff Vale Railway K class 0-6-0 No. 3, as it stands at Cardiff Cathays shed. Designed by Hurry-Riches, and built at Kitsons and TVR own works, between 1874 and 1889, they started life as the L class, being rebuilt from c1889. They had $17\frac{1}{2}$in x 26in cylinders, 140psi boiler pressure, 4ft $6\frac{1}{2}$in wheels, 17,380lbs T.E. and weighed $36\frac{1}{2}$ tons, ideal for the mineral trains they hauled.

This broadside picture of K class No. 58, again at Cardiff Cathays, shows the weather shield on the tender to protect crews when running tender first, a regular occurrence on the TVR. Altogether there were 85 of these locomotives, several of which passed on to the GWR, with the last being withdrawn in 1930.

The TVR was predominantly a mineral railway, and although tank engines later dominated the scene, 0-6-0s were widely used during the last century. Typical of the earlier varieties of this type of engine is No. 252, dating from c1860, having 16in x 24in cylinders and 140psi boiler pressure. It stands on the shed roads at Cardiff Cathays still shining, despite its age.

This delightfully quaint looking I class 4-4-0T, No. 68, built at Cardiff in 1884, stands among the typical debris of a steam shed, at Cardiff Cathays. They had 16in x 24in cylinders, 140psi boiler pressure and 5ft 3in driving wheels, and originally had half cabs. As befits their ornate external appearance, these were used on the passenger services, and were later fitted for push-pull working. All three engines were passed onto the GWR, but were withdrawn by 1925.

The six engines in Hurry-Riches C class were the first inside cylinder 4-4-2Ts built in Britain. No. 171, built at the Vulcan Foundry in 1888, rests in another view at Cardiff Cathays. Having $17\frac{1}{2}$in x 26in cylinders, 160psi boiler pressure, 5ft 3in driving wheels, 17,195lbs T.E. and weighing 54 tons, they were used for the 'valleys' passenger services and, compared with the I class, were an altogether more purposeful looking engine. They were all scrapped 1925–7.

The crew of the almost brand new O3 class 0-6-2T No. 55, built at the Vulcan Foundry in 1905, have a quick pose for the camera while waiting at Cardiff Cathays. These had $17\frac{1}{2}$in x 26in cylinders, 160psi boiler pressure, 4ft 6in driving wheels, 19,870lbs T.E. and weighed 63 tons, making them ideal engines to haul the endless stream of coal trains on the TVR.

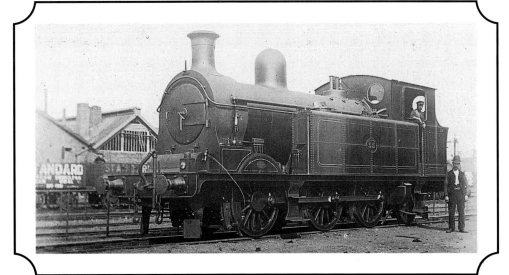

Perhaps the most interesting of this series of photographs taken at Cardiff Cathays, shows the crew of U1 class No. 197, built at the Vulcan Foundry in 1896, busily preparing the engine for its next duties. Of particular interest is the array of oil cans, used to lubricate all the necessary parts of a steam engine. These 0-6-2Ts had 17$\frac{1}{2}$in x 26in cylinders, 160psi boiler pressure, 5ft 3in driving wheels, 17,190lbs T.E. and weighed 63 tons, and were used on both passenger and coal trains. In 1921, 150 out of 271 TVR engines were 0-6-2Ts, but wholesale scrapping soon began, once the GWR had decided on a standardised replacement for all the Welsh 'valleys' companies' engines.

This view of Pontypridd captures the atmosphere of the Welsh 'valleys' in their heyday. Pontypridd was one of the busiest stations in South Wales, perhaps the busiest, although most of the traffic was generated by the then extensive coal industry. A passenger train enters the station, hauled by one of the ubiquitous tank engines, amidst typical 'valleys' scenery.

Third class 0-2-2 steam rail-car No. 11, built by Kerr, Stuart & Co. at Stoke-on-Trent in 1905, awaits its next duty at Cardiff. These were introduced on the Cardiff–Cadoxton services in 1903, and were quite successful. Nevertheless, the fluctuating nature of South Wales passenger traffic was not really suited to the restricted loading of these trains, and they were not widely used.

Rhymney Railway

Founded in 1854 to build lines from Rhymney to Hengoed, connecting with the GWR to Newport, and Rhymney to Cardiff, joining the TVR, the RR became another prosperous 'valleys' railway. Like the other companies in this area, coal was the main source of revenue, and the competitive rivalry for this lucrative traffic was fierce.

The RR became closely linked with the Bute family, and their Cardiff docks. This inevitably led to conflicts with the TVR, and in 1871 the RR opened its own line to that major port. By 1884, the RR had an alternative route to Newport, via Caerphilly and the BMTJctR. This was important as, in all the political toing and froing, the RR had incurred the wrath of the GWR, by allying itself with the LNWR, and allowing the latter access to Merthyr.

As with the majority of smaller railways, engines on the Rhymney Railway tended to have an extended life on the important duties, whereas they would have been displaced onto secondary duties much earlier, on a large railway. This elderly 0-6-0, No. 14 seen at Cardiff, is one such example of this. It continued to work coal trains well into this century, making quite a contrast with the modern designs.

Lundie's double-framed A class 2-4-2T No. 64, built in 1890 and seen here at Cardiff, shows the diversity of designs used before the 0-6-2T came to dominate South Wales services. These had 17½in x 24in cylinders, 150psi boiler pressure, 5ft driving wheels, 15,620lbs T.E. and weighted 54 tons 8 cwt. The obvious lack of adhesion from this wheel arrangement soon rendered it obsolete on coal trains; however, they continued to be used on passenger services and other light duties. The last one was withdrawn in 1928, but No. 64 was rebuilt as an L1 class 0-6-2ST in 1911, being withdrawn twelve years later.

Having its own locomotive works at Caerphilly, the RR was a fairly self-contained company, though typical, in most respects, of others based in South Wales. C. T. Hurry-Riches, son of the TVR Locomotive Superintendent, took charge at Caerphilly in 1906, and eventually the 0-6-2T came to dominate the engine scene; the older types, such as those portrayed, being gradually withdrawn. Nevertheless, these dark green engines, with their brown frames, remained quite distinctive until Grouping, and the absorption into the GWR. It says much for the nature of its traffic, that the RR, having 51 route miles of its own, possessed more locomotives, with 121, than coaches.

From being a bit of an outcast among the little railways of South Wales, the RR came to be seen as little different to the norm for the area, as it made its peace with its neighbours. The RR was never as wealthy as the TVR, nor as friendly as the BMTJctR, but sat somewhere in between the two, maintaining healthy profits, while providing good local services.

Brecon & Merthyr Tydfil Junction Railway

Of all the important Welsh valleys railways, this was the least profitable, arriving rather late on the scene. Incorporated in 1859, and having the section from Dowlais to Brecon opened in 1863, the BMTJctR can ultimately trace its ancestry back to 1826, when the Rhumney Railway opened, which it absorbed in 1863. The main line ran from Brecon to Newport, although the BMTJctR only owned 26 of the 47 route miles. Needless to say, the BMTJctR was dependent on the goodwill of its rivals, and this was not always forthcoming in the hot-house of severe railway competition that was the Welsh valleys. At one time or another this plucky little railway was involved in conflicts with the GWR, RR, TVR and LNWR, and lived a rather precarious existence as something of a local 'punch-bag'.

Operating in the north and east of the Welsh coalfield, the docks at Newport was the intended destination for much of the company's freight traffic. The steeply graded lines were ideally suited to tank engine operation and from 1890 all trains were thus worked. Like many small railways the locomotives were purchased elsewhere, to BMTJctR designs. J. T. Simpson was the first Locomotive Superintendent, followed by T. Mann, 1869-73. C. Long reigned 1873–88, and G. C. Dunn continued the good work until 1909. As one would expect, nothing spectacular was produced, but neither was there room for expensive mistakes, so all designs were up to the job in hand, if by and large following the trends established by the rival companies.

Unprofitable the railway might have been, but unfriendly it most certainly was not. Guards' names were printed in the working timetable, and loyalty amongst staff was second to none. This characterful railway steadfastly maintained its independence, until absorbed by the GWR in 1923, and its idiosyncrasies and inefficiencies were sadly lost.

C. Long designed 0-6-0ST No. 18 for the Brecon & Merthyr Tydfil Junction Railway, was built in 1881 by Sharp, Stewart & Co., and it survived until 1932, having covered over one million miles with only one change of boiler. It wore No. 11 until 1889, and is seen here at Newport, beside some heavily dressed ladies. Having 17in x 24in cylinders, 140psi boiler pressure, 4ft 6in wheels, 14,870lbs T.E. and weighing 38 tons, it was a very useful 'all-rounder' engine for this steeply graded railway.

By tank engine standards, G. C. Dunn's 2-4-0T No. 25, built by Stephenson in 1898, had a short life, being withdrawn in 1922. With 16in x 24in cylinders, 150psi boiler pressure, 5ft driving wheels, 13,055lbs T.E. and weighing 43 tons, it worked Newport–Brecon passenger trains. Looking a much older design than it was, it is seen here at Newport before beginning another double-headed 'thrash' up to Brecon; it certainly did not lead an easy life.

Alexandra (Newport & South Wales) Docks & Railway

In terms of route mileage, with only nine miles, this was the smallest of the main South Wales railways. Yet its importance is shown by it having over 100 miles of track on Newport docks, working regularly over 13 miles of other companies' routes, and having running powers over a further 88 route miles.

Dating back to the incorporation of Newport docks in 1835 and opened in 1842, the Alexandra (Newport) Dock Co. was incorporated in 1865, but the cost of building the new dock caused the company to fail. The dock was completed though, and in 1882 the title name was adopted.

Five engines to this design were purchased by the Alexandra (Newport & South Wales) Docks & Railway from Stephenson, in 1898. They had 16in x 24in cylinders, 150psi boiler pressure, 4ft 0½in wheels, 16,320lbs T.E. and weighed 40 tons. They were withdrawn between 1925 and 1929, but as this picture shows, were well cared for, despite their mundane docks duties.

A close working partnership was established with the BMTJctR and the expansion of business through the Alexandra Dock, principally coal exports, was rapid. In 1897 it took over the Pontypridd, Caerphilly & Newport Railway (opened 1884), which ensured the continued existence of traffic from the heart of TVR territory.

Naturally, with the majority of its track being on the dock estates, the tank engines, particularly the 0-6-0ST, was the main form of motive power. These were all bought from locomotive builders, and served the company until absorbed by the GWR in 1923. Thereafter, many were sold to mining companies and worked out lives of varying lengths.

Despite having to rely on other railways bringing the coal from the pits, the A(NSW)DR continued to prosper. As with all South Wales railways, this was heavily dependent on the export of coal. Prior to World War One, Britain had a dominating position on the world markets for that product, but the 1920s saw a major decline, as world trade slumped and British coal became less competitively priced. All the South Wales lines suffered a sharp decline in such traffic, and the docks at Newport were often a distressing sight to those who had worked on this once ebullient, busy little concern, especially during the Edwardian days.

The contemporary standards of care and attention that were lavished on even dock tanks, is amply shown here as No. 15, built by Robert Stephenson in 1885, is prepared for the day's work. It had 18in x 24in cylinders, 150psi boiler pressure, 4ft 6in wheels, 18,360lbs T.E. weighed 46³/₄ tons, and was withdrawn in 1929. The attention given to engines at this time, reflected company pride and loyalty.

No. 19 with outside cylinders, was one of two 0-6-0STs purchased from Peckett & Sons (Bristol) to one of their standard designs, in 1891. Having 14in x 20in cyclinders, 140psi boiler pressure, 3ft 6in wheels, 11,105lbs T. E. and weighing 26 tons, it was ideal for light, dock shunting, duties. It became GWR No. 680, and was finally scrapped in 1949. Its sister engine, No. 18, was sold by the GWR in 1929, and survived until 1953, working at a colliery. No. 19 is seen busy shunting at Newport, exhibiting cans, brushes and chains above its wheels.

Cambrian Railways

This railway was centred on, ironically, Oswestry (Salop.), where it had its workshops and was, with nearly 300 route miles, the only Welsh railway that could be regarded as a 'system'. Formed in 1864 through the amalgamation of five companies, the Cambrian ran from Wrexham and Whitchurch to Aberystwyth and Pwllheli, and south from Newtown to Brecon. It even included the Welshpool & Llanfair and Vale of Rheidol narrow gauge railways, and ran through some of the most desolate, yet beautiful, country to be found anywhere. There is little doubt that this aspect of the Cambrian enhanced its popularity, and formed a good basis for tourist business.

Until the 1890s the Cambrian was noted for neither punctuality nor efficiency, and the arduous nature of many of its lines in Wales meant that speeds were generally low, even for those far-off days. Traffic, especially in Wales, was sparse, although the through routes in England helped the financial situation. Towards the end of the 19th century, tourist traffic from the Midlands developed and, with this, came better connections with the neighbouring GWR and LNWR.

Having good workshops at Oswestry, the railway built many of its own locomotives. A. Walker, 1864–82, was the first Locomotive Superintendent, designing the successful and pretty 'Beaconsfield' class, the premier engines of the line. William Aston held the post until 1899 with Herbert Jones carrying on until Grouping in 1922. As can be seen in the photographs, great pride was taken in the condition of the locomotives, a feature of railways large and small at that time.

Very much a rural railway, the Cambrian maintained the best aspects of this type of system and yet had a 'main line' character. In this respect it was certainly unique among the Welsh railways.

The four engines which comprised the 'Beaconsfield' class were the principal passenger engines of the Cambrian Railways. They had 17in x 24in cylinders, 140psi boiler pressure, 5ft 6½in driving wheels, 12,410lbs T.E. and weighed 33 tons, and were the first engines on the railway fitted with vacuum brakes. No. 20, built in 1886, bears the hallmarks of the traditional British 4-4-0 as it poses for the camera. It was rebuilt in 1914, and withdrawn eight years later.

The crew of No. 90, built in 1903 by Stephenson, is busy making final adjustments before continuing the journey. H. E. James designed the 89 class, and they had 18in x 26in cylinders, 170psi boiler pressure, 5ft 1½in wheels, 18,630lbs T.E. and weighed 41 tons 13 cwt. They cost £2,730 each, a large amount for the time, and No. 90 was withdrawn as early as 1922, but others survived until 1954. Though principally goods engines, the class occasionally worked passenger trains, and could operate over all the Cambrian main lines.

London & South Western Railway

Of the constituent companies that formed the Southern Railway at the 1923 Grouping, the LSWR was the one which most resembled the other large railways in Britain. Like all railways operating into London, it had a large and financially important commuter patronage; but unlike the LBSCR or SECR, the LSWR ran long distance expresses comparable to those of other railways. As with its southern rivals though, goods traffic was very much of secondary consideration to the passenger business. Thus, it had to be quite innovative in attracting passengers to the line, when for some of the northern railways they were regarded as a bit of a nuisance, getting in the way of the prolific and profitable goods traffic. The LSWR performed its tasks well though, paying the fourth highest dividends to shareholders, out of the ten largest railways, during this century. This was a fine reflection of the way the LSWR handled its important staple traffic.

From obtaining its Act of Parliament in 1834, the London & Southampton Railway was seen by northern railways as the 'champion' of the 'standard gauge' cause in the South, against the emerging GWR and its allies, which used the 'broad gauge'. The main line from London was built via Basingstoke, to act as a springboard for a standard gauge alternative route to Bristol. The line to Southampton was opened in stages, being completed in 1840, but the title of the company was changed to the LSWR the year before, due to a branch being opened from Eastleigh to Gosport. Rivalry between the towns of Southampton and Portsmouth, being as keen then as it is now, pushed the railway into a corner, from which a neutral title was the only sensible means of escape.

The next two decades saw the LSWR expanding rapidly, although not always building the lines itself. By the end of the 'railway mania', in 1848, it had a new London terminus, at Waterloo, reached Salisbury via Eastleigh and Dorchester via Wimborne. The remote Bodmin & Wadebridge Railway in Cornwall, was also, illegally, purchased, to become a pawn in the battle against the GWR in later years. By 1860, with a more direct route to Portsmouth via Havant, the LSWR had protected its eastern flank from penetration by the LBSCR, leaving it free to attack GWR territory. The LSWR took the battle to the GWR by entering Weymouth and then, although not reaching Bristol, by opening the line from Basingstoke to Exeter. The rest of the 19th century seemed to be spent either building, or buying, lines in the West Country, much to the chagrin of the GWR.

It was this never-ending battle for influence in the West with the GWR, which illuminated the history of the LSWR. Before the end of the century, the LSWR had reached Bath and the Somerset coast, thanks to a joint line with the MR; and punched across the GWR line at Exeter, to reach Plymouth, Ilfracombe, Torrington and on into North Cornwall at Bude and Padstow. Thus, the 'withered arm' of the lines west of Exeter was completed. Needless to say, the GWR was not happy about the situation, but as the LSWR trains had to run over GWR metals at both Plymouth and Exeter, there was always going to be a bit of jiggery-pokery between the two railways. There were all sorts of arguments and counter-arguments regarding unnecessary delays, particularly at Exeter, and relations remained strained between the two companies and their employees until Grouping, and even into BR days.

Not that the LSWR had been idle in its own territory. A direct line to Bournemouth from Southampton, via Christchurch, ultimately shortened the distance to Weymouth and offered a clear advantage over the GWR route from London. Most importantly, in 1892, the company bought the docks at Southampton, and began to expand these to become the fulcrum of the goods services.

The LSWR could certainly be classified as an 'expansionist' railway, not beneath a bit of under-hand dealing, when deemed necessary. Yet the contemporary and historical image of the LSWR is more like that associated with the Kings of Wessex, when fighting the marauding Danes; they had 'right' on their side. Though the 'good' image had much to do with the 'battle of the gauges', the proximity of alternatives to most of its routes ensured that standards of services were high.

The first Locomotive Superintendent, Mr J. Woods, purchased engines from outside builders, but John Gooch, the brother of the GWR's Daniel, built the first engines, at the Nine Elms Works, in 1846. He left

Opposite top: The 21 engines of Adams 460 class 4-4-0 for the LSWR were built by Stephenson and Neilson between 1884 and 1887, the last gaining a gold medal at the 1887 Jubilee Exhibition at Newcastle. They had 18in x 24in cylinders, 160psi boiler pressure, 6ft 7in driving wheels, 17.6 sq ft grate, weighed 46 tons, and proved to be excellent performers on West of England and Southampton line expresses, being both fast and economical. Towards the end of the century they worked the Exeter–Salisbury semi-fasts, and were also to be found on the Portsmouth line. Later still, some were transferred to Cornwall/Devon services until withdrawal in the 1920s, proving both popular and reliable performers with trains far removed from those for which they were designed. No. 466, built in 1884, awaits departure from Waterloo with a South Coast express, having had its Adams stovepipe chimney replaced by a standard Drummond type. Its elegant and classic lines make quite a contrast to the grimy appearance of the station. It was withdrawn in 1928.

Middle: This unusual view shows Drummond mixed traffic S11 class 4-4-0 No. 397, built in 1903, at Waterloo. Known as "Small Bulldogs" they had 19in x 26in cylinders, 175psi boiler pressure, 6ft 1in driving wheels and weighed 52 tons, being designed for Salisbury–Exeter expresses. They spent most of their time in the West Country, but some appeared on Portsmouth line expresses before 1914, and again during the period 1921–6, with all ten being shedded at Fratton at one time. Between 1941 and 1945 the whole class was transferred to the LMS, mostly to work on the SDR section, but also throughout the LMS system as well. Nine were withdrawn in 1950, but No. 400 survived until 1955, on the Reading–Redhill line.

Below right: Drummond's "Big Bulldog", L12 class 4-4-0 was an express version of the S11 class, with similar dimensions except for having 6ft 7in driving wheels and weighing 55 tons. They worked Bournemouth/West Country expresses in their early days, being capable of reaching 80mph, and No. 421 was involved in the Salisbury accident of 1906. No. 433, built in 1904/5, is seen at Nine Elms when new, looking every inch a typical Drummond design of this period. This engine was transferred with nine others of the class to the South Eastern section in 1925, to work Dover expresses; some returned there in the 1930s. Eighteen were withdrawn in 1951, but the last survived until 1955 on the Reading–Redhill line.

for the ECR in 1850, and for the next 28 years the Father and Son of the Beattie family held sway. Their engines were well up to the mark, if not outstanding, but it was the appointment of William Adams from the GER in 1878, which took the LSWR to the top of the locomotive tree. As can be seen from some of the pictures, Adams' engines were both graceful and powerful for the time. It was during Adams' tenure in office, that the LSWR effectively established itself as a serious, effective rival to the GWR.

No less a character, and feared Victorian autocrat, than Dugald Drummond succeeded Adams. His record with the NBR and CR, was mightily impressive, possibly to the point of raising expectations too much. His earlier 4-4-0s added to his excellent record of designs, and the express C8 and T9 classes, and mixed traffic K10, L11 and S11 classes, were right to the forefront of contemporary British locomotive practice. It is sad to relate, therefore, that his later 4-6-0 designs

were never quite up to the work expected of them, and were modified by the old firebrand's successor, Robert Urie. One lasting, highly successful legacy of Drummond's was the final moving of the works from Nine Elms to Eastleigh, after decades of indecision.

Exeter Queen St. (later Central) was always full of activity, with trains being split for several destinations, and engines being changed. Here, an L11 class awaits the arrival of an express from London, to take its portion forward into Devon. Forty engines were built 1903–7 and had 18½in x 26in cylinders, 175psi boiler pressure, 5ft 7in driving wheels and weighed 46 tons, with 32 tons for adhesion. Despite being known as "Grasshoppers", due to their tendency to slip, these engines worked well on secondary duties, particularly in the South West. Some worked Waterloo–Reading services, until that line was electrified in 1939, and all were withdrawn between 1949 and 1952.

Below right: Apart from being a benevolent autocrat with regards to employees, Dugald Drummond was an engineer who continually tried to improve his designs. Following a prototype, built in 1897, he designed the five engines that comprised the E10 class 4-2-2-0s in 1901, with two pairs of single driving wheels. These had (4) 14in x 26in H.P. cylinders, with the inside cylinders driving the leading wheels, and the outside cylinders the rear wheels, 175psi boiler pressure, 24.7 sq ft grate, 6ft 7in driving wheels and weighed 54½ tons. They were poor steamers, prone to slipping and were not popular with the crews, being used only when Nine Elms was short of engines. However, they were quite free running under favourable conditions. No. 369 is seen at Nine Elms with its crew, presumably discussing the job to be done. The last one was withdrawn in 1927.

Adams A12 class 'Jubilee' 0-4-2s, built 1887–95, were similar to the 'Gladstones' of the LBSCR, though not as elegant. Unlike those, the 'Jubilees' were mixed-traffic engines, but they enjoyed a distinguished and lengthy life. Thirty-one survived World War II, due to locomotive shortages, and the last four were scrapped in 1948. They had 18in x 26in cylinders, 160psi boiler pressure, 6ft driving wheels, 15,850lbs T.E. and weighed 43 tons. This view of Nine Elms shows No. 533, built in 1887, with the Shed Foreman and No. 197 behind. The 'Jubilees' were used on a wide variety of services until Grouping, including excursions, West Country passenger, fast goods to Southampton and the West of England, and semi-fast services into London.*

By this century then, the LSWR, running trains from the hurly-burly of suburban London, to the wild and remote parts of Cornwall and Devon, had established itself in the 'second division' of British railways. Its main source of revenue was from the passenger services, whether for commuters, long distance, holiday makers or service personnel. Perhaps it was because of this, that the LSWR enjoyed such a favourable reputation. Then there was the shipping interests and, with Plymouth and Southampton docks, direct connections with the prestigious trans-Atlantic crossings. Also, some of the London suburban routes were electrified, thus raising standards still further. The LSWR had always been a go-ahead railway and, unlike other competitors, had never felt confined, or shackled, to South East England.

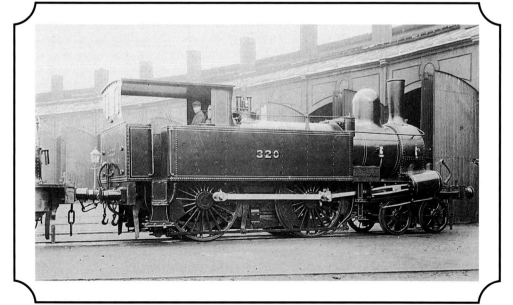

Beattie ordered six 'Metropolitan' type 4-4-0T engines from Beyer Peacock in 1875 to work the newly opened Exeter–Plymouth route. Known as "Plymouth tanks", the 318 class had 17in x 24in cylinders, 120psi boiler pressure, 5ft 9in driving wheels and weighed 44 tons. They were far from ideal for such duties, having an inadequate coal and water carrying capacity, and were soon sent to work the Leatherhead services. No. 320 makes a quaint sight at Nine Elms, partially rebuilt by Adams. The whole class ended its days working around the New Forest, and was withdrawn between 1906 and 1914, with No. 320 being the last.

The 59 engines of Adams O2 class were built 1889–95, and some survived until the end of steam on the Southern Region of BR. With 18in x 24in cylinders, 160psi boiler pressure, 4ft 10in driving wheels, 17,235lbs T.E. and weighing 47 tons, they were ideal for light branch and suburban passenger work. The class worked throughout the LSWR, and later on the Central Section of the SR, proving to be very popular with crews. Virtual immortality came in 1923 when 23 engines were renumbered, given names and transferred to the Isle of Wight. For the next 40-odd years, they were synonymous with the island, and steamed their way into the hearts of thousands of visitors and locals alike. No. 229, built in 1891 rests among a line of engines at Nine Elms. It was withdrawn in 1961. Forty-eight O2s passed on to BR, while 18 survived on the Isle of Wight, to 1964; a marvellous testimony to their designer.

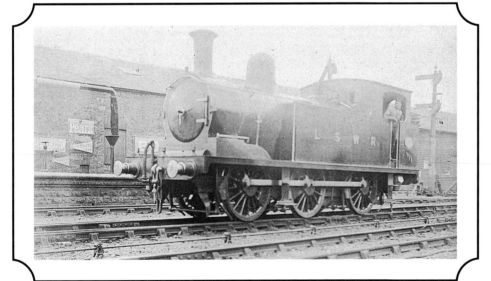

Adams G6 class 0-6-0T, built between 1893 and 1900, was designed for shunting and short-haul goods traffic. An unidentified engine is seen waiting in the centre road of Exeter Queen St. These were used to assist trains up the hill from St Davids station for many years, often working in pairs or even in threes. They had 17$^{1}/_{2}$in x 24in cylinders, 160psi boiler pressure, 4ft 10in wheels, 17,230lbs T.E. and weighed 46$^{3}/_{4}$ tons. Twenty-four of these were built after Adams retired, and were slightly modified by Drummond, reputedly not being as free steaming. All 34 were withdrawn during the period 1948–62.

Lynton & Barnstaple Railway

In many ways this 1ft 11$\frac{1}{2}$in gauge railway was a cameo of a typical small British railway company. In two important respects it was certainly representative: namely, under-capitalisation and fervent employee loyalty. As was, and still is, far too often the case, the company managed to survive through the 'devotion' to duty of its staff. However, the unexpected cost of construction was to be an ever-tightening noose around the neck of the company, which finally throttled its life away.

The aim had been a laudable one, to link the small towns of Lynton and Lynmouth, with Barnstaple and the rest of Britain. As so often happened with British railway companies, the cost of construction exceeded expectations. The line left Barnstaple at sea level and rose to over 1,000ft before descending to a terminus 700ft above Lynmouth the town that it purported to serve, also at sea level. All this in a distance of 19$\frac{1}{2}$ miles. Several cuttings and the need to hack the route out of the side of rocky hills ensured that costs were high.

From the opening in 1898 the Lynton & Barnstaple used three Manning, Wardle 2-6-2Ts. The next year, a 2-4-2T was bought from the Baldwin Co. of USA, copying several main line companies, following the strike by the Amalgamated Society of Engineers. These engines worked the L&BR until it was absorbed into the Southern Railway in 1923.

Unfortunately, despite useful summer traffic, the railway never paid its way, and the premier English narrow gauge railway closed in 1935.

Though this picture has an historical interest, in showing Lynton station on the Lynton & Barnstaple Railway, it is one of the most disappointing in the whole collection as it is quite 'lifeless'. This picture shows the northern terminus during the first years of its life. There is little activity either on the station or around the engine shed, but this would have been an accurate reflection of life for much of the day.

London, Brighton & South Coast Railway

People commuting into London by rail, have suffered greatly down the years. Whatever the railway, whether it was one of the pre-Grouping companies, or BR, under the guise of either the regions, or Network SouthEast, it has had to endure the not always good natured derision towards its services, from the 'regulars'. The LBSCR suffered more than most, primarily because for much of the 19th century it was a downright incompetent railway, but also because such a high proportion of its passengers were commuters. Like BR today, this was the company the commuters loved to hate but, unlike BR with its mostly new, or refurbished stock, the LBSCR treated its regulars to some of the most antiquated and unreliable trains to be run by a major railway in Britain.

A remarkable transformation took place, so that by the Edwardian era the LBSCR was one of the most popular railways in the land. Its stylish, yet quaint-looking engines, usually in the pink of condition, bore names which conjured up a certain 'adventure', or 'romance', about travel, like *Bordeaux* and *Boxhill*. Its trains, though never fast, were expected to be punctual, and were as much a part of a commuter's life as was the place of work, the two inextricably linked together. This was also the railway the "Sunny South Specials" aimed for from the North; the eager trippers being disgorged at Brighton, Bognor, Hastings and Eastbourne. Nevertheless, whether on business or pleasure, the LBSCR seemed to exist for passengers, and not goods.

The London & Croydon Railway opened a line from the London & Greenwich Railway–West Croydon, in 1839. The London & Brighton Railway built a joint line with the SER to Redhill, and opened its own line on to Brighton in 1841. This confusing and congested situation, which saw four railway companies' trains using the same lines between London Bridge and New Cross, was a result of the government wanting only one railway line out of London to the South; there is far-sightedness for you, which shows that it is not just recent governments that are incapable of any form of planning, among other things. All sorts of schemes were tried to improve matter, like 'pooling' locomotives, but the ever-increasing traffic only made things worse. In 1845 an attempted amalgamation between the SER, LSWR, LBrR and LCR failed, but the latter two joined to form the LBSCR the following year.

In 1846 the coastal line from Brighton to Hastings opened, and the Brighton–Portsmouth line followed shortly afterwards. Further expansion in rural Sussex was undertaken during the next two decades, and with the opening of a brand new London terminus at Victoria in 1860, jointly owned with the LCDR, the limit of LBSCR building was virtually reached.

Hemmed in by the SER and LCDR to the east, and the LSWR to the west, its Portsmouth and Hastings services were subjected to severe competition. However, apart from the 'Battle of Havant' in 1858, when gangs of platelayers and other employees of the rival LBSCR and LSWR companies fought over the latter's right to use the LBSCR lines from Havant to Portsmouth, a form of mutual co-existence seemed to prevail.

As previously mentioned, the reputation of the LBSCR, with regard to its train services, was extremely poor. Away from the main London–Brighton line, the trains were slow, and 'punctuality' did not seem to be part of the staff vocabulary. Furthermore, the coaches tended to be uncomfortable and old, and were hauled by the most diverse, unreliable bunch of engines imaginable. Many stations, unusual for the mid-19th century, were often maintained in an unkempt condition, adding to the aura of a badly run railway.

This wholly unsatisfactory situation began to improve with the appointment of William Stroudley as Locomotive Superintendent, from the HR, in 1870. Prior to this there had been four previous incumbents, the most notable being J. C. Craven, who lasted 22 years. It was Craven who transferred the locomotive works from New Cross to Brighton, the first engine being built there in 1852. Stroudley inherited an awesome 72 different locomotive designs, with few locomotives in good condition, and the majority being incapable of carrying out the work required of them.

These ancient engines were allowed to be run into the ground, and Stroudley concentrated on new, standardised designs. Many of these had a magnificent appearance, were well cared for, and were more than masters of the work. A policy of one driver/one engine was pursued, giving staff a certain 'pride' in their work. Unfortunately, this was more of a publicity exercise, as the Running Department was still poor; the bright engines could not hide reality.

R. J. Billinton replaced Stroudley in 1890 and, during his 14 years in office, he introduced the first bogie-wheeled engines on the railway. Douglas Earle Marsh, from the GNR, succeeded Billinton in 1905, and designed the first 'Atlantic' engines. These were nearly identical to Ivatt's design on the GNR, and certainly improved the express services. Finally, L. B. Billinton, son of the former chief, took over in 1911, until Grouping.

Perhaps the man most responsible for improving the 'reality' of the LBSCR services, was Mr Forbes, who became the General Manager in 1899, and later served on the Board. With a more than adequate locomotive stock, and improved coaches, he set about putting that expensive equipment to use by improving punctuality and reliability, and also tidying up the system, particularly the stations. Within a commendably short time the LBSCR became a 'model' of efficiency, and a shining example of how a good railway should be run.

In 1908 Victoria station was doubled in size, and the following year the South London services were electrified. The 'Brighton's' transformation seemed complete. Here was a railway with a huge commuter load, serving many sleepy country stations, which had achieved a degree of popularity envied by many other railways. This was, no doubt, aided by the fact the LBSCR served such fashionable towns as Brighton, Hastings and Eastbourne. A good reputation has to be earned though, and there is little doubt that the LBSCR was deserving of such, from the 1890s onwards.

W. Stroudley designed the first two G class 2-2-2s in 1874 for the LBSCR, followed by 24 more between 1880 and 1882. They were primarily intended for the Portsmouth line services, and were not displaced from this difficult route until after 1895. They had 17in x 24in cylinders, 140psi (later 150psi) boiler pressure, 6ft 6in driving wheels, 10,600lbs T.E. and weighed 33 tons, but despite their diminutive size, they were highly successful engines. No. 330 Newhaven, built in 1881, is seen here at Brighton, after being relegated to secondary duties. In May 1907, three engines were sold to the Italian State Railways.

Stroudley's most famous design was the B, or 'Gladstone', class of which 36 engines were built after 1882. Despite their unusual 0-4-2 wheel arrangement the class successfully, and glamorously, hauled the principal expresses to Eastbourne, Brighton and Portsmouth for many years. They had 18$\frac{1}{4}$in x 26in cylinders, 140psi (later 150psi) boiler pressure, 20.6 sq ft grate, 6ft 6in driving wheels and weighed 38 tons, with 28 tons for adhesion. The driver of No. 200 Beresford seems to be troubled by a problem from underneath the engine, while standing at Croydon, in 1899.

'Gladstone' class No. 217 Northcote *later No. 670, built in 1883, is entering Croydon with a 'down' express. When displaced off the express services early this century, the 'Gladstones' performed reliably for many years on secondary passenger duties, unlike many contemporary 'singles'. Eight survived into the 1930s, the last being withdrawn in 1933, with No. 214* Gladstone *being the first locomotive to be secured for preservation by a railway society.*

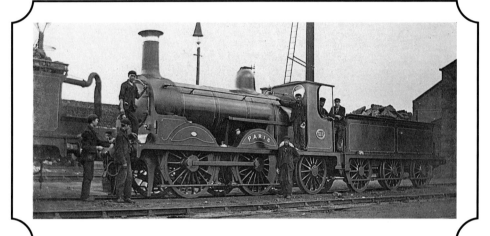

Seven people pose for the camera at Newhaven shed, around D2 class No. 313 Paris, *built in 1883. Stroudley first tried the 0-4-2 wheel arrangement on this design, and 14 engines were built between 1876 and 1883. They had 17in x 24in cylinders, 140psi boiler pressure, 5ft 6in driving wheels, 12,500lbs T.E. and weighed 34 tons. As mixed traffic engines, their most noteworthy duties were the Worthing–London fast fruit trains, and the London–Newhaven express goods trains.*

Stroudley's successor, R. J. Billinton, reverted to more traditional wheel arrangements for his engine designs. His B4 class 4-4-0s of 1899–1902, proved to be reasonably successful express passenger engines, and numbered 33 in total. No. 61 Ladysmith, *built in 1901, is receiving attention at Croydon from the fireman, while hauling a London bound train. In 1903 No. 70* Holyrood, *ran the 51 miles from London to Brighton in 48³/₄ minutes, with a Pullman train.*

B4 class No. 49 Duchess of Norfolk, *built in 1901, was originally named* Queensland, *and is seen here at Croydon. The B4 class was more useful than outstanding, but undertook sterling work for over 30 years. They had 19in x 26in cylinders, 180psi boiler pressure, 6ft 9in driving wheels, 16,750lbs T.E. and weighed 50 tons. Their names began to be removed from 1906 due to a change in policy under the regime of Douglas Earle Marsh, appointed as Locomotive Superintendent the previous year.*

Billinton's initial 4-4-0 passenger design, the B2 class, was not particularly successful. Twenty-five engines were built between 1895–98, and the need for larger boilers was immediately apparent. They were soon rebuilt, and designated the B2x class, with 18in x 26in cylinders, 160psi boiler pressure, and 6ft 9in driving wheels, though they were neither particularly free-steaming, nor powerful engines, and mainly worked lightweight express trains. No. 316 Goldsmid, *built in 1895, is approaching Croydon with a Portsmouth express.*

A fine display of advertisements accompany this picture of Stroudley's E class 0-6-0T No. 98 Marseilles, *built in 1874. Seventy-two engines were built between 1874 and 1883, and with 17in x 24in cylinders, 140psi (later 150psi) boiler pressure, 4ft 6in wheels and weighing 39^1/$_2$ tons, they were a 'goods' version of the D class. Several heavily rebuilt examples survived until the 1960s.*

Billinton's first design was the D3 class 0-4-4T, of which 36 were built between 1892 and 1896. They had 18in x 26in cylinders, 170psi boiler pressure, 5ft 6in driving wheels, 17,435lbs T.E and weighed 52 tons 17 cwt. No. 383 Three Bridges, *built in 1893, rattles through Old Kent Road, with a mixed set of coaches. Wooden platforms, lamps and advertisements are of particular interest.*

D3 class No. 371 Angmering, *built in 1892, is being prepared for its day's work at New Cross. There is quite an array of tools on the top of the water tank, all performing a necessary task in the daily life of the steam engine.*

Billinton continually developed Stroudley's E class design, and the E4 class radial 0-6-2 tanks, of which 75 were built between 1897 and 1903, were particularly useful. Having 18in x 26in cylinders, 160psi boiler pressure, 5ft driving wheels, 19,100lbs T.E. and weighing 52 tons 12 cwt, they worked on passenger services, but were very versatile. All were scrapped between 1944 and 1963 except No. 473 Birch Grove, *now preserved on the Bluebell Railway. No. 498* Strettington, *built in 1900, is on the turntable at Brighton.*

One of the most successful of all LBSCR tank engine designs was Stroudley's D class 0-4-2Ts, 135 of which were built between 1873 and 1887. With 17in x 24in cylinders, 140psi boiler pressure, 5ft 6in driving wheels, 12,500lbs T.E. and weighing 38$^{1}/_{2}$ tons, their duties ranged from light expresses and Brighton semi-fasts, to heavy goods trains. About 50 were later permanently attached to coaches, forming push-pull trains. No. 243 Ovingdean, built in 1881, rests at New Cross.

This typical shed scene, at Newhaven, features No. 419 (in the olive green goods livery) of Stroudley's C class 0-6-0, his first design for the LBSCR, built between 1871 and 1874. They had 17$^{1}/_{4}$in x 24in cylinders, 140psi boiler pressure, 5ft wheels and weighed 35$^{5}/_{8}$ tons, but these do not reveal the relative modernity of the class. All 20 were scrapped 1901–4.

South Eastern & Chatham Railway

Perhaps of most interest today, with regards the pre-Grouping railways, is the wide and varied backgrounds of the many companies that formed the major transport system of this country during the last century. Each company had its own traditions, characteristics, practices, alliances and rivals. Often routes were duplicated, which resulted in fierce competition between the opponents, but seldom can such a ridiculous situation have existed as that between the South Eastern Railway, and the London, Chatham & Dover Railway. Nearly all that was bad about laissez-faire government policy, with regards to a transport network, was all too apparent in the relationship between these two erstwhile rivals. That these two companies were able to form a joint management committee and to co-operate, although never formally amalgamate, in 1899, would hardly have been foreseen only a few years prior to the event.

The SER, by first leasing the Canterbury & Whitstable Railway (which opened four months before the Liverpool & Manchester Railway), in 1844, and then buying it nine years later, dates back to 1830. That line was engineered by Robert Stephenson, and made a ridiculous deviation to include an unnecessary tunnel, as the promoters wanted one! Stephenson also provided the one locomotive to be used, *Invicta*, the twentieth to be built by that renowned firm.

Also incorporated into the SER was the London & Greenwich Railway, opened, from what is now London Bridge station, in 1838. It was the first railway in London, and the first 'overhead' railway in the world, as it ran on long sections of arches. This was important more for the fact that the SER obtained its first terminus station, rather than the line itself.

By 1844, using running powers and joint lines from London to Redhill, Dover was reached, via Tonbridge and Folkestone. The section from Redhill to Ashford was both straight and level, the whole route being engineered by Sir William Cubitt. Two years later a line from Ashford to Ramsgate, via Canterbury and Margate was opened, and in 1849 the Redhill–Reading line was purchased, which offered a through route to the GWR.

Expansion slowed considerably, and the last major route, to Hastings, was opened in 1852. Competition with the LCDR forced the opening of a shorter route from London to Tonbridge via Sevenoaks, in 1868. Prior to that, two new London termini were opened, at Charing Cross and Cannon St., which provided much needed space, and direct access to the City of London. With a growing number of maritime services to Europe, the SER seemed to be in a very secure position.

Ashford Works was opened in 1847 and the first engine was built there in 1853. James Cudworth was the first Locomotive Superintendent, 1845–76, but his locomotives were a rather weak and piecemeal bunch. Two successors lasted barely two years, and in 1878 James Stirling, brother of the GNR's Patrick, moved south from a similar position on the G&SWR. Within 20 years, Stirling had transformed a ramshackle locomotive stud into perhaps the most standardised in the country, all bearing the familiar Stirling cab and dome-less boiler.

The domineering personality of the SER though, was Edward Watkin, who reigned as Chairman from 1866 to 1894. He simultaneously held the same position the MSLR and MetR, and was a very aggressive competitor as far as the LCDR went. The three companies which Watkin chaired formed the backbone of his dream of trains running direct from France, via a Channel tunnel, to the North of England. Though this failed to materialise, he was the driving force behind the 'London Extension' of the GCR, and his far-sighted plan has finally come to fruition, albeit using different routes.

The LCDR was never in the same league as the SER, and yet it not only survived but, much to Watkin's chagrin, flourished gaily. Its origins date to the formation of the East Kent Railway in 1853, and it became the LCDR six years later. Opening in a very fragmented fashion, its own line from London Victoria to Dover was completed in 1863, along with the Faversham–Margate section.

The LCDR was fortunate in gaining the Royal Mails contract, which the SER had refused, thus promoting its Channel steamer services. This was doubly important, as by 1866 the LCDR was in the hands of the Receiver. However, despite what Watkin would have liked to see, the LCDR survived under the leadership, and later Chairman, of Mr James Forbes. He was also the Chairman of the Metropolitan District Railway, a fierce rival of Watkin's Metropolitan Railway, and so there was little love lost between these two forceful characters.

The LCDR main line to Dover was far more difficult to work than the SER route. It was an endless succession of steep gradients, and average speeds were low. The first two Locomotive Superintendents, C. R. Sacre, later of Watkin's MSLR, and Mr Quadley, had both been sacked by 1860. William Martley followed, until he retired in 1874, and some of his engines were highly successful on both Dover trains, and London suburban services. The final Locomotive Superintendent was William Kirtley, nephew of the MR incumbent; during the 19th century, there were several examples of members of one family holding such a position on different railways, like the Stirling's Gooch's, Worsdell's, and Beatties among others.

Nepotism, what is that? Although he did not standardise to the same extent as did Stirling on the SER, Kirtley designed many distinguished engines, of which his M3 class was possibly the best. Nevertheless, the LCDR continued to 'borrow' locomotives, particularly from the GNR.

When the Managing Committee was formed in 1899, the reputation of the two constituent companies with the passengers was poor, in the extreme. Trains were made up of all sorts of odds-and-ends of coaches, and the popular nickname for the poor old LCDR, of 'Load'em, smash'em and over' railway, was certainly justified. The track of both main lines was the worst

out of London, and contributed both its fair share to the LCDR nickname, and the popular SER title of the 'slow and easy railway'. Harry Wainwright took over as the new Locomotive Superintendent, and gradually centred all locomotive building and repairs at the Ashford works of the SER, the LCDR works at Longhedge eventually closing. He was to prove the ideal person to undertake such an onerous task.

Modernisation was both an essential, and enormous task, yet within 15 years the SECR was one of the best railways in Britain. A great example that co-operation, and not needless competition, will reap the most benefits for all concerned.

The SER 259 class 2-4-0s of 1876, was designed by Ramsbottom of the LNWR, and was very similar to his 'Newton' class. Twenty were built by the Avonside Engine Co. and Sharp, Stewart, but unlike the 'Newtons', they were not a great success and were soon demoted to local duties. They had 17in x 24in cylinders, 120psi boiler pressure, 6ft 6in driving wheels, weighed 29 tons, and were solid, reliable engines, known as "Ironclads". The front end of No. 271 is shown in detail as it stands with some well dressed men at Bricklayers Arms, after being rebuilt, minus dome, by Stirling. An R class 0-6-0T with cut down cab, stands behind.

J. Stirling's O class, for the SER, was highly successful, and 122 were built between 1878 and 1899. They had 18in x 26in cylinders, 150psi boiler pressure, 5ft 2in wheels, 16,100lbs T.E. weighed 41 tons and nearly all were rebuilt by H. Wainwright. Many passed onto BR, the last being withdrawn in 1960. No. 388, built in 1893, rests at Bricklayers Arms, early in the SECR days.

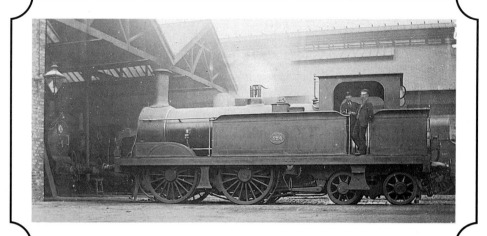

Another Stirling standard design for the SER was the Q class, of which 118 were built between 1881 and 1897, for passenger duties. No. 324, built by Neilson in 1882, is at Bricklayers Arms, with its crew. These 0-4-4Ts had 18in x 26in cylinders, 140psi boiler pressure, 5ft 6in driving wheels, 15,150lbs T.E. and weighed 46¼ tons. Rebuilding as the Q1 class began in 1914, and domes were fitted to the boilers. Despite this, all were withdrawn by 1930.

Stirling's least numerous standard design was the R class, of which 25 were built between 1888 and 1898, for branch working. Many were rebuilt by Wainwright as the R1 class, 1910–22. Nine of these passed onto BR, many surviving on the Folkestone Harbour branch, and elsewhere, into the 1960s. The rebuilds had 18in x 26in cylinders, 160psi boiler pressure, 5ft 2in wheels, 18,480lbs T.E. and weighed 46¾ tons. No. 128, built in 1892, is seen at Bricklayers Arms in its new colours, with a cut down cab for working the Canterbury–Whistable branch.

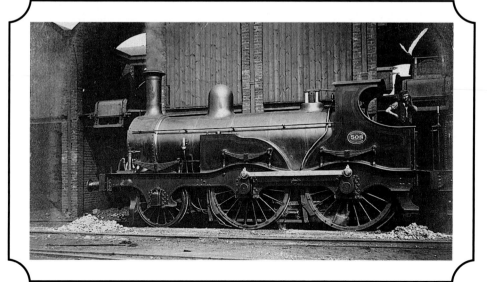

On the formation of the SECR, the SER engines kept their former numbers, while the LCDR engines had 459 added to theirs. Thus LCDR No. 49, originally named Zephyr, became SECR No. 508, and is seen here at Longhedge with its tired driver, during its twilight years. This was the last of six built by Thomas Brassey to W. Martley's design in 1865, to replace the Crampton 4-4-0s on the express trains. They had 16in x 24in cylinders, 120psi boiler pressure and 6ft 6in driving wheels. The other five had a sandbox around the lower part of the dome to keep the sand dry, but fortunately, No. 508's lines have not been so spoiled.

M. Kirtley's M3 class 4-4-0s for the LCDR numbered 26 engines, one built in 1880, and the rest between 1892 and 1901. No. 476 (LCDR No. 17), built 1894, is passing Rochester with the 3.20pm ex-Victoria. With 18in x 26in cylinders, 150psi boiler pressure, 6ft 6in driving wheels, 13,750lbs T.E. and weighing 42¹/₂ tons, they were notably free running engines. Along with the earlier M class variants, they worked the Kent Coast and Continental traffic over the ex-LCDR lines well into this century.

Martley's last design was the C class 0-4-2T "Long-backed Scotchmen", of which six were built, these being a larger version of Sturrock's "Scotchmen" on the GNR. They worked on London suburban lines for over 40 years, including the Victoria–Moorgate–Wood Green GNR/Hendon MR services. They had 17in x 24in cylinders, 140psi boiler pressure and 5ft 7in driving wheels. No. 558 Mona (LCDR No. 99), built in 1873, rests in the wide spaces of Longhedge, before it was rebuilt.

Kirtley's first modern design was the A class of 1875, which was the first of a long line of LCDR/SECR 0-4-4Ts, and they were the most powerful tank engines in Britain when introduced. They had 17¹/₂in x 26in cylinders, 140psi (later 150psi) boiler pressure and 5ft 3in driving wheels, being used on the intensive London suburban services. Seen in its LCDR days, No. 112 stands at Longhedge with an ancient tank engine visible beyond. All were withdrawn between 1923 and 1926.

Kirtley designed the T class for shunting duties in 1879. Two were built then, and eight more between 1889 and 1893, with three passing on to BR, being scrapped in 1951. They had 17½in x 24in cylinders, 160psi boiler pressure, 4ft 6in wheels, 18,510lbs T.E. and weighed 40¾ tons. No. 608 (LCDR No. 149), built in 1889, is seen in yet another view taken at Longhedge. This was the works of the LCDR, but was downgraded after the SECR was formed, and closed by 1911.

The classic lines of Wainwright's D class, built 1901-7, are shown to good effect by No. 733, built in 1901, on the turntable at Longhedge. They had 19in x 26in cylinders, 175psi boiler pressure, 6ft 8in driving wheels, 17,450lbs T.E., weighed 50 tons and worked Kent and Continental expresses for many years. Twenty were later rebuilt by R. E. Maunsell as the D1 class, but 48 out of 51 passed on to BR, and were very popular engines. In their latter years, they graced various cross-country services, like the Ashford–Hastings route. No. 733 was withdrawn in 1957, but fortunately No. 737 has been preserved.

The first new design for the SECR was the C class 0-6-0 goods engines, of 1900–8. As with many designs for the South East routes, they were solid and dependable, rather than technically innovative. They had 18½in x 26in cylinders, 160psi boiler pressure, 5ft 2in wheels, 19,420lbs T.E. and weighed 43¾ tons. The majority passed on to BR, and several survived into the 1960s, occasionally working branch passenger trains. No. 38, built in 1902, is at Bricklayers Arms.

Midland & Great Northern Joint Railway

This railway, formed in 1893, was unique in that it was jointly owned by two railway companies who were rivals in most respects, the GNR and MR, and yet it maintained a very separate identity. It dates back to the Norwich & Spalding Railway of 1853, but most of the other companies that formed the MGNJtR, like the Lynn & Fakenham Railway, were not authorised until the 1870s.

The main line began as an end-on junction with the MR at Castle Bytham, near the GNR main line, with another section running from the GNR at Peterborough to meet up at Sutton Bridge, and made its way across the fens and north Norfolk to Great Yarmouth. There were branches to Norwich and Cromer, both leaving the main line at Melton Constable, home of the locomotive works.

William Marriot was appointed as Locomotive Superintendent of the Eastern & Midland Railway, itself an amalgam of three smaller companies, in 1884 and he held that post until 1924. He was something of a likeable demi-god in his sphere of influence, although locomotives continued to be supplied by outside builders to the designs of GNR and MR engineers until 1900.

Most of the passenger traffic was directed to Great Yarmouth and originated from the MR and GNR, this latter company even running trains to Cromer direct from King's Cross. There was, of course, much competition with the GER for the holiday, fish and agricultural traffic. However, locally sourced revenue was always inadequate.

Perhaps most surprising of all though, and what James Grimoldby would never have imagined when he first took pictures of MGNJtR engines, was that this company would remain in existence for many years after all its contemporaries were but a memory, having become part of a 'Big Four' company. Equally sad, is that little remains of this system today, its obliteration being more complete than almost any other English Railway.

Former Lynn & Fakenham Railway A class 4-4-0, built in 1881, and seen here as MGNJtR No. 24, is at Great Yarmouth. This had 17in x 24in cylinders, 140psi boiler pressure, 6ft driving wheels, 10,789lbs T.E. and weighed 38½ tons, with 24 tons 6 cwt for adhesion. Built by Beyer Peacock it was noticeably similar to Adams 4-4-0s for the LSWR, and likewise Johnson's inside cylinder 4-4-0s for the MR. It was also a very successful engine, and hauled the principal passenger trains for over 40 years.

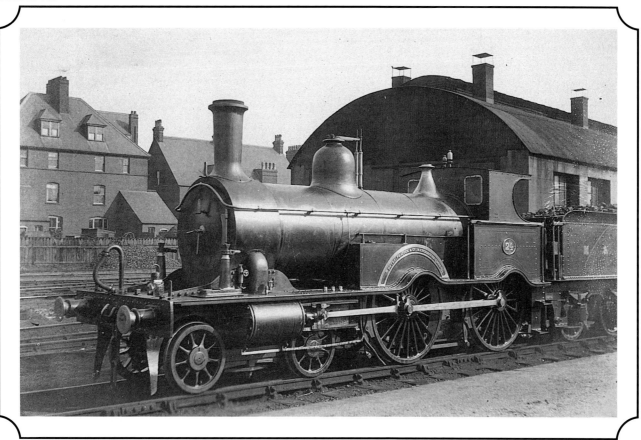

Metropolitan Railway

The public opening of the world's first underground railway took place on 10th January 1863, on the 3¾ miles of broad gauge line between Paddington (Bishop's Rd) and Farringdon St. The service provided was quite intensive right from the start, there being 67 trains in each direction daily, at 15-minute intervals. Trains did not run 'during church hours' on a Sunday, a folly which survived until 1909.

Initial plans to link the GWR with the Eastern Counties Railway, at Shoreditch, dated from 1845, but it was not until after the success of the Great Exhibition in 1851, that matters were, at last, put in hand. The Bayswater, Paddington & Holborn Bridge Railway was formed in 1853, and became the North Metropolitan Railway later that year. Surprisingly, considering the alleged pioneering spirit of the entrepreneurial class of those times, capital was difficult to raise, and sufficient amounts were not obtained until 1859. Once underway, building was hampered by flooding, exploding gas mains and other such eventualities, but the line was completed by mid-1862, only to be flooded once again!

The MetR was operated by the GWR until mid-1863 when, due to a number of disputes, the GNR and LNWR stepped in at short notice to provide standard gauge coaches and engines. Peace was quickly made with the GWR and some broad gauge trains reappeared, but the last ones ran in 1869.

The success of the new 'underground' railway quickly led to plans being laid to build an 'inner circle'. A second company, the Metropolitan District Railway, built a line from South Kensington round the south of central London, while the MetR extended eastwards to Aldgate. The MDR was operated by the MetR until 1871, but another dispute flared up to end that arrangement. The 'inner circle' was not finished until 1884, and an Act of Parliament was required to force the two companies to operate services over each other's track.

The MetR also had ambitions of becoming a main line railway, and an extension from Baker St to Finchley Rd was begun in 1868. Progress in building the new line was slow, and Harrow was not reached until 1880, but under the chairmanship of Edward Watkin, a plan to link up a route from the North of England to France, via a Channel tunnel, was hatched. As we know, this did not happen but the GCR eventually reached London, via joint lines with the MetR, and the latter acquired lines from Aylesbury to Verney Junction, over 50 miles from Baker St.

After the dispute with the GWR, the MetR ordered its own distinctive, condensing 4-4-0T engines from Beyer Peacock. These engines worked the 'circle' until it was electrified in 1905, little altered from the original design. Larger engines began to appear for the 'extension' lines, but these hard working Beyer Peacock tank engines came to personify the Metropolitan.

Grouping, in 1923, left the MetR untouched. It was absorbed into the London Passenger Transport Board in 1933, despite opposing the plan, along with the other London underground and bus companies.

A Metropolitan Railway train for New Cross is approaching Farringdon, behind Beyer Peacock built 4-4-0T No. 47. This design dates from 1875, but is essentially an updating of the original 1863 design. A member of the crew is sitting precariously on the bunker of the engine. The third coach in the train is of interest, whilst another train emerges from the GNR/MR tunnels to the far left. These fascinating engines worked all over the country when sold by the MetR, after it was electrified.

Millwall Extension Railway

Of all the railway companies featured in this book, this is the most peculiar. A little known, or indeed cared about, railway, the territory it served has once again come to prominence with the emergence of the Docklands Light Railway, and the £250m one-mile long road tunnel (who says the Department of Transport does not favour road over rail?).

Parliamentary permission was sought for the London, Blackwall & Millwall Extension Railway, which was granted in 1865. It was promoted by the London & Blackwall Railway and the Millwall Canal Company, which was building the new Millwall Docks, to run from Millwall Junction, on the LBR, to North Greenwich, on the Isle of Dogs. The new dock opened in 1868, and the railway followed, as far as Millwall Dock station, three years later, reaching North Greenwich in 1872. From there, until 1902 when the walkway under the River Thames was opened, a ferry operated to Greenwich.

By far the most unusual facet of the MER was the ownership of the route. For those readers not familiar with the vagaries of imperial measurement, there are 80 chains to a mile, ie one chain = 22 yards. The first 5 chains from Millwall Junction station were owned by the LBR; the next 42 chains belonged to the East & West India Docks Co.; the following 52 chains belonged to the Millwall Dock Co.; with the final 31 chains owned by the LBR. The line was lightly built, as steam engines were not used due to the fire risk when passing through the various docks, and consisted of

Millwall Extension Railway 'coffee pot' No. 6, waits at Millwall Junction prior to setting off with yet another train for North Greenwich. Three of these diminutive 2-4-0T engines were built by Manning, Wardle in 1880, for the introduction of the intensive steam hauled passenger service. These cheeky looking engines had 9in x 18in cylinders, 120psi boiler pressure, 5 sq ft grate, 3ft 6in driving wheels, 261 sq ft heating surface area and weighed only 16 tons. No. 6 was rebuilt by the East Ferry Road Engine Co. in 1907 and, when the MER was absorbed into the PLA in 1909, was renumbered No. 31. These engines often carried advertisements for Pears Soap on their tanks, at various times. The spark arrester, to reduce the fire risk in the wood yards, is clearly visible, as is the 'coffee pot' on the firebox. Their humdrum lives came to an end in 1922, when replaced by former GWR steam railcars.

single track, with a passing loop at South Dock station, where the company had its headquarters.

From the beginning, it was proposed to run a passenger service at 15-minute intervals, until 6.30 pm when it became half-hourly; the Sunday service also ran every 30 minutes. All trains were horse drawn until 1880, which created just as many operational problems as did the closure of the isolated South Dock station, on the India Docks property, at 6.30 pm each day.

Then, in 1880, the whole line was strengthened in a modest way, and a steam engine service was introduced. Eventually, twelve engines were purchased between 1873 and 1901; three 2-4-0Ts in 1880 for the passenger trains, and nine 0-4-0Ts for shunting on the docks. The passenger trains worked on the 'two engines in steam' system, and were made up of two or three ancient coaches loaned by the GER, successor to the LBR. The drivers were former dockers, provided by the Millwall Docks, and the guards were supplied by the GER.

Life trundled along its merry way, with little of consequence affecting the company. Perhaps the 1889 dock strike might have upset things a bit, but road competition was restricted, and in any case, the stations were on the docks they served. Between 1901 and 1910 Millwall Rovers F.C. played their home football games at Millwall, and on match days traffic was boosted by five-coach trains of football supporters;

with their recent reputation, one wonders how the frail, ancient coaches would have stood up to the onslaught faced today.

In 1909 the Port of London Authority was formed by an amalgamation of The London & India Docks, The Millwall Dock Co. and The Surrey Commercial Dock Co. The MER became part of this new company, but despite occasional disruptions during World War One, life carried on much as before. By the 1920s the passenger engines, and ancient coaches in particular, had deteriorated markedly, and were replaced by former GWR steam railcars.

The economic depressions of the 1920s took their toll on both the docks and the railway, and passenger and goods traffic steadily declined. During the General Strike in 1926, the PLA ended the passenger services, never to restart. It seems as though the PLA made the most capital out of this opportunist moment, to avoid the potential hoo-haa of going through the proper procedure. Goods services carried on for a few years afterwards, but even these were dwindling, and closure became inevitable.

Thus ended the mundane existence of this odd little railway, best remembered for its diminutive passenger engines. It had clearly served the Isle of Dogs well for over 50 years, and it was a rather sad, not to say dishonest, way of securing its closure. Perhaps the MER would be pleased to consider the Docklands Light Railway its spiritual successor.

Great Southern & Western Railway

Of all the multitudinous railways operating in the Emerald Isle, this was both the largest by far, and the only one comparable to some of the 'giants' operating on mainland Britain. Expectations of this railway were quite different to those operating elsewhere in the four provinces: passengers expected trains to run on time, and not to be left 'stranded' as no engine was available; goods and parcels were expected to arrive at their destinations, and not to have 'vanished' en route; workers expected a reasonable standard of living, and not to be told the company had no funds for wages; and shareholders expected a return on their investments, and not excuses, followed by false promises for

the future. It was indeed, a tall order for a railway operating in such a sparsely populated, poor country.

As ever, the GtSWR's beginnings were modest enough; a Dublin–Cashel railway, hopefully extending to Cork at a later date. Building work began in 1845, but Cashel was by-passed, with Cork being reached four years later. This, of course, was the period of the Irish 'Potato blight', when hundreds of thousands starved to death through a combination of a diseased potato crop, (the 'staple' diet), English 'laissez-faire' government and English, virtual 'feudal', colonial rule. Hundreds of thousands more emigrated to Britain, Europe and especially the USA, to escape either death, or an oppressed, deprived existence. It says much, therefore, that an English aristocrat, Lord Bentinck, went to the House of Commons to appeal for funds to employ 50,000 navvies to build the Dublin–Cork line, and to help relieve the famine.

At first, most expansion was around Cork and Dublin, but by the 1860s the GtSWR had lines running from Limerick to Tralee, and on to the Kerry peninsula from Killarney. It had established connections with the WLWR, and although its great rival was the MGWR, the GtSWR was an efficient operation.

Compared with other railways in Ireland, the GtSWR was an excellent employer. Though maintaining a strict discipline with its staff, it paid high wages, gave more than a passing thought to staff welfare, for example having its own school at Inchicore, and was rewarded with high morale among the staff. Obviously, this was reflected in the high standards of service offered to passengers, something not normally associated with Irish railways in the 19th century.

By 1901, when it took over the WLWR, the GtSWR dominated the area south of the Dublin–Galway line except, of course, the south-east corner, and pierced the rival MGWR territory, with the line up through Galway to Sligo. The route mileage was about 1,500, not far behind the MR in England, although most of it was single track.

The Inchicore Works, in Dublin, was opened in 1849 and, although 40 engines were purchased in England, the first locomotive was built there in 1852. Alex McDonnell arrived as Locomotive Superintendent in 1864 and he standardised designs, giving engines a family resemblance, while keeping costs down. He also had an astute eye for future engineering talent, as he recruited John Aspinall from Crewe in 1875, who left in 1886 to take charge of LYR locomotive design, and Henry Ivatt, also from Crewe, in 1877, as his assistants. Both of these took charge of locomotive design at Inchicore in their own right, before Ivatt left to go to the GNR in 1896. Robert Coey was recruited to replace Aspinall, and he took charge when Ivatt departed. By that time the GtSWR had nearly 250 engines, mostly of modern design, of which well over three quarters had been built at Inchicore. As such, the GtSWR was more than a match for the majority of British railways, and far ahead of its Irish competitors in locomotive matters.

This was a complete railway, offering a comprehensive service throughout its extensive network. Early this century the GtSWR owned something over one third of all route miles of Irish railways, and was twice the size of its nearest rival. Its network of main lines has managed to survive the ravages of the war of independence, the civil war, grouping, nationalisation and competition from the motor car, incidents which have driven many other Irish lines out of existence. That its lines have survived thus far, and forms the rump of today's Irish Rail, says much about the ambitions and operations of the GtSWR.

This scene, at the 5ft 3in gauge Great Southern & Western Railway Inchicore shed, features Ireland's most common engine, McDonnell's 101, or J15, class 0-6-0 of 1873, which eventually numbered 119 examples, most of which were built at Inchicore Works. They had 18in x 24in cylinders, 140psi boiler pressure, 5ft 1¼in wheels and weighed 30¾ tons. Many later received Aspinall's 160psi boiler, and in the 1930s a number were again rebuilt, receiving a Belpaire firebox and superheaters. The last engines were withdrawn in 1960, and the class was equally at home on goods and secondary passenger duties. No. 188 can be seen along with sister engine No. 170, being prepared in the background, with another similar engine inside the shed.

In 1869 McDonnell designed some 2-4-0s not dissimilar to contemporary LNWR engines. They had 16in (1875 ones 17in) x 22in cylinders, 140psi boiler pressure, 6ft 7in driving wheels, weighed 30 tons and were used on the Dublin–Cork expresses. No. 74 approaches Cork with one of these trains, amid a backdrop still recognisable today. Loads were modest in Ireland, and this enabled these diminutive engines to enjoy a long life hauling these principal expresses.

The GtSWR had several branch lines in the remote south-west corner of Ireland, and it was for these that four 4-4-2Ts were built in 1900. They have a contemporary appearance, and with 17in x 22in cylinders, 160psi boiler pressure, 5ft 8¹/2n driving wheels and weighing 54 tons, were well up to the mark compared to other British designs. No. 27 is at Tralee, terminus of the infamous narrow gauge Tralee & Dingle Light Railway, with a mixed train and attendant complement of railway workers.

Waterford, Limerick & Western Railway

Few of the Irish railways were very profitable and, of the larger companies, this was one of the poorest. The English GWR took an interest in the WLWR, so as to have a partner in offering an alternative to the rival LNWR and DWWR route to Dublin, via Holyhead. The various subsequent loans from the GWR, helped the WLWR to survive on several occasions.

The WLWR paid low wages, occasionally cutting these further, kept maintenance to an absolute minimum, and would often cancel services, rather than pay for a borrowed locomotive, if one of their own had failed. Naturally, staff morale was low, and the services suffered as a consequence. Nevertheless, despite the poor financial situation, the WLWR expanded steadily through a combination of takeovers and amalgamations.

The Waterford & Limerick Railway was the first in

Ireland to obtain an Act of Parliament, in 1826. A line from Limerick to Tipperary was opened in 1848, and reached Waterford in 1854. It expanded south-west to Tralee by 1850 and, with great audacity, eventually reached Sligo, driving through the MGWR 'sphere of influence', by taking over smaller railways.

This 'poor relation' had built up quite a route mileage, but it remained badly run. William Malcolmson took control, and the company began to adopt a more 'professional' approach. He tried to boost patronage by introducing fourth class return fares at 1½ times the single price, only you travelled in

open wagons! He slightly negated this though, by not wanting trains to run on Sundays. Yet, despite efforts such as this, the rural nature of much of the country, through which its lines travelled, ensured that the WLWR remained poverty stricken.

The WLWR was courted by the mighty GtSWR, mainly because of its route mileage, and especially the line through MGWR territory to Sligo. In 1901 this maverick railway amalgamated with, and was absorbed by the GtSWR, thus passing its problems onto its former rival. Perhaps the ultimate way of affecting GtSWR performance?

The Waterford, Limerick & Western Railway possessed eight of these 2-4-0s, designed by J. G. Robinson (later of the GCR), for its main line Waterford–Limerick services. They had 17in x 24in cylinders, 150psi boiler pressure, 6ft driving wheels and weighed 36½ tons. No. 20 Galtee More, *built in 1892, is entering Limerick with a mixed train from Waterford, past the goods sheds and loading sidings. The Irish 5ft 3in gauge is emphasised by this low-level photograph.*

J. G. Robinson designed these 0-6-0s for main line goods services, and eight were built by Kitson between 1897 and 1899. They had 17in x 24in cylinders and 5ft 2in wheels, but No. 2 Shannon, *seen here on the grandiose shed at Limerick, was the only one to receive a Belpaire firebox. An older 0-6-0, No. 20, rests in the background.*

Dublin, Wicklow & Wexford Railway

Formed as the Waterford, Wexford, Wicklow & Dublin Railway in 1846, and later renamed the Dublin & Wexford Railway, the line opened between Dublin and Bray in 1854. Two years later it leased the Dublin & Kingstown Railway, the first Irish railway to run steam-hauled passenger trains, in 1834, and took over its services. In 1859 a more central station in Dublin, at Harcourt St. was built.

While never a wealthy concern, expansion continued southwards, reaching Wexford in the 1860s; taking over the Wexford & Rosslare Railway in 1898, and finally reaching Waterford, via GtSWR lines, in 1901. To celebrate this event, having taken over 50 years, the name was changed, once again, to the Dublin & South Eastern Railway. However, due to competition from trams in Dublin, no more dividends were paid after 1901, but fortunate shareholders of the DKR were still being paid 9% interest, quite an investment in those times of falling prices, when the pound was 'as good as gold'.

Train services were mostly local, but Bray, near Dublin, was developed as a resort. Also, the company handled most of the traffic from England, via the ports of Kingstown (Dun Laoghaire) and Rosslare. As with most of Ireland's railways, there were few long distance trains and they tended to be slow. Hence motive power needs were modest.

Unpretentious though it was, with only 160 route miles, the DWWR was one of the larger Irish railways and was quite distinctive to its mighty neighbour, the GtSWR.

Water pours from the side tank of No. 60 Earl of Courtown, *after it has been replenished. This 2-4-2T was built by the LNWR at Crewe, but was bought by the Dublin Wicklow & Western Railway and converted to the Irish gauge.*

A Dublin bound train, headed by tank engine No. 11, enters the busy station of Bray. The Irish railways tradition of using a single platform for trains running in both directions, rarely used in England, can be seen in operation. The most renowned example of this was the maverick workings at Limerick Junction, where untold contortions were made to allow trains to stop there.

Midland Great Western Railway

Irish railways were usually very different from their English counterparts, and the MGWR followed this pattern, at least in its early years. Authorised in 1845 to build a line from Dublin to Mullingar, this section opened in 1848, and was extended to Galway in 1851. The 126-mile journey took well over five hours, by the fast train! Later expansions took lines out to Sligo, Clifden, Westport and Achill, all on the west coast.

Despite this continued expansion, the MGWR was badly rundown by the 1860s, with its services bearing no relation to the timetable, that is if they ran at all! Staff morale was at a low ebb, and corruption amongst the many directors was rife. An Englishman, Joseph Tatlow, was employed as the General Manager at that time, and under his direction the company greatly improved its services, continued expanding by taking over smaller railways, and became profitable.

As Ireland was divided into 'spheres of influence', with regards to railways, so there were many disputes with its larger neighbour, the GtSWR. However, traffic in western and central Ireland was never so great that these problems could not be overcome and, eventually, good working relations were established.

By 1900, the transformation was complete, and the MGWR, with its emerald green engines, was the third largest in Ireland. The days when the luckless Lord Chancellor waited in vain for his train to start, only to be told by the guard, "it couldn't get started any sooner if you were the County Court Judge himself", were over. Of course, it did not last. Other major problems soon emerged with which all railways were forced to grapple; the war of independence.

M. Atcock's D class 2-4-0, of which twelve were built by Neilson in 1873, for the Midland Great Western Railway, No. 21 Swift *passes a westbound train as it approaches Dublin Broadstone. They had 15in x 22in cylinders, 5ft 7in driving wheels, and were used for the main line passenger services.* Swift, *and four sister engines, worked the slower Sligo and Mayo line trains for many years, lasting well into this century. The rather ancient coaches emphasise the extra width of the Irish gauge.*

Isle of Man Railway

'Time waits for no man', but of all the railways in this book, 'time' has stood still for the IMR, at least regarding locomotives, coaches and stations. The only real difference between the IMR when new and now, apart from line closures, is that it is now primarily a 'tourist attraction', and not a true 'working' railway.

Unlike many other British narrow gauge railways, the IMR was a main line in miniature. It had junction stations, a grandiose terminus station, engine works and sheds, signal boxes and 'fast', as well as 'slow', trains. It worked to a regular timetable, conveyed parcels, newspapers and miscellaneous goods traffic, and the whole operation was little different to that of a major mainland railway.

Incorporated in 1870, the Douglas–Peel line opened in 1873, followed by the Douglas–Port Erin line the next year. The 3ft gauge was large enough to handle hefty traffic, yet small enough to keep costs down.

In 1879 the Manx Northern Railway opened a line of the same gauge from St John's, on the Peel line, to Ramsey in the North. These two companies worked closely from the beginning, and through trains between Douglas and Ramsey started in 1881. One further line, from St John's to Foxdale, was opened in 1883 by the Foxdale Railway, owned by the MNR, to exploit the local minerals.

At the end of the century the Manx Electric Railway opened throughout from Douglas to Ramsey, and gave stiff competition to the MNR. The IMR eventually took over the MNR and FoxR, in 1905, and the service was maintained until the 1960s.

Locomotives on the IMR were all 2-4-0Ts, of steadily increasing size, built by Beyer Peacock, between 1873 and 1926. The MNR had four engines, three virtually the same as the IMR's, and a Dübs-built 0-6-0T for the Foxdale line. At least on paper, nearly all of these still exist today.

On many occasions a double-headed train of ancient four and eight-wheeler coaches could be seen, with up to a thousand passengers on board, pounding between Douglas and Port Erin. The lines to Peel and Ramsey were more rural in nature, offering a certain amount of tranquillity, and quite a contrast, just like a 'real' railway. Which is what the IMR was. Today you can still savour this railway system in miniature. True, it is mainly a passenger railway, depending on tourism, but the IMR is still as unique as the Manx cat.

Isle of Man Railway No. 7 Tynwald, *built in 1880, enters Port Erin with a train from Douglas watched by a schoolboy and a quaintly dressed girl. These 3ft gauge Beyer Peacock built 2-4-0Ts varied only in detail during their 53 years of building, from 1873, and they all had 3ft 9in driving wheels and weighed about 20 tons. At the height of the busy summer workings double-headed trains carrying up to one thousand 'packed' passengers, were not uncommon on this little railway.*

Jersey Railway

"Mad dogs and Englishmen" is a colloquialism which holds a fair amount of truth, at times. It could certainly, with hindsight, be applied to many railway building projects; what other country, confined to such a small island, would have well over one hundred separate railway companies operating in the age of the motor car? One answer could be the island of Jersey. Measuring ten miles by six miles at the extremities, no less than four unrelated railways were being planned for Jersey during the 1870s. Three of these were actually under construction during that decade, and two became fully operational concerns. To those of us used, nowadays, to huge national concerns, this sort of competition really does seem like madness.

The JR operated west from the capital, St Helier, along the coast to St Aubin. Plans for a railway to connect these places were first considered in 1845 but, as with many railways, matters ended there and then. They were revived 15 years later and, after a further wait of a mere nine years, permission was granted to build. Though the line was only 3³/₄ miles long, and single track, it was opened to traffic in the autumn of the following year, a remarkably short time considering previous rates of progress.

Initially, the lightly built standard gauge line was operated by two Sharp, Stewart built 2-4-0Ts, joined by two more a year or so later. The coaches were either open or closed four-wheelers, their use depending upon the season of the year. Traffic picked up during the 1870s and the JR even opened its own hotel at St Aubin, but by 1874 the railway was in serious financial straits. Thereafter, ownership seemed to change with each passing season, without any general improvement in either services, or the financial position, a portent of BR franchising?

Concurrently with all that, the St Aubin's & La Moye Railway & Granite Quarries Ltd was intending to build a railway, from some quarries in the south west to St Aubin. As is the way with these things, landowners of the proposed route realised they could be in for a financial killing, and the prices they asked just about did for the whole project. A sense of reason eventually prevailed, and by 1877 the first rails were laid, to a gauge of 3ft 6in. However, the financial position of that company deteriorated dramatically during the year, and all construction had stopped by December, despite the first two locomotives having been purchased.

There matters rested until, in 1883, after both the aforementioned railways had changed hands on several further occasions, they were purchased by a consortium headed by Viscount Ranelagh. Construction of the unfinished La Moye line was begun and, surprisingly, the following year the JR was converted to the 3ft 6in gauge. Two engines were purchased to work the line, and in 1885 the hitherto separate railways were connected at St Aubin, allowing a through run from St Helier to Corbiere, a distance of 7³/₄ miles; "All that fuss over nothing", is the saying that springs to mind.

The first few years of the enlarged company went quite well, although the hoped-for goods traffic never materialised. The company changed hands on a few further occasions, but such 'fun and games' was becoming commonplace. Then, days after celebrating the 25th anniversary of the opening, the company, appropriately, went into liquidation! In 1896 the Jersey Railways & Tramways Ltd took over the JR and began to initiate improvements, although nothing more was heard of the 'trams'. These 'improvements' included buying another engine, shortening the route and rebuilding St Helier station. This time, at long last, the change of ownership, and subsequent alterations, began to have a positive effect for all concerned. The financial position improved, and dividends were paid until World War One, of 2-3% pa.

During that stable period the JRT ran a regular daily service throughout the year. Coaches were of the bogie type, all fully enclosed. Trains were usually formed of three coaches, both First and Second class, and a four-wheeled brake. Later, in 1923, the first of four steam railcars were purchased, as was a bus company, which acted as a 'feeder' to the rail services.

The decade of the 1920s proved to be 'roaring' for the JRT; passengers reached the one million mark in 1924/5, receipts soared and dividends of over 5% pa were paid. However, the decline, when it came, was rapid; winter services were cut out, and receipts slumped. A fire put the JRT out of its misery in 1936, a dramatic and fitting end to the turbulent life of this little railway. The Nazi German occupiers of World War Two saw fit to have a railway line constructed on the island, but the inhabitants today must feel that they have managed to imprison themselves in a concentration camp with tarmac as fencing, patrolled by cars as guards. There are more cars per mile in Jersey than anywhere else in Europe today, and on such a tiny island. What price the revival of the JRT now?

In readiness for the reopening with a 3ft 6in gauge, the Jersey Railway purchased two 2-4-0Ts from Manning Wardle in 1884. One of these, No. 1 St Heliers, has just been uncoupled from its train after arriving at St Helier. These had 13in x 18in cylinders, 140psi boiler pressure, 3ft 6in driving wheels and weighed 25 tons. No. 1 enjoyed a full life, being rebuilt in 1910, and then remaining in service until the JRT finally ceased to operated. Unfortunately it was scrapped in 1937.

Jersey Eastern Railway

Encouraged by the successful launch of the Jersey Railway, plans were soon afoot to build a railway eastwards from St Helier to Gorey. Permission was granted in 1871, work began the following year and the whole route was completed, after a few hiccoughs, in 1873: conception to opening in just 2½ years. That was in complete contrast to the drawn out performance required in building the JR, and thereafter, the two railways pursued totally different paths.

As mentioned in the relevant section, the JR changed ownership as often as some people change their hats. On the way to the 'glorious 1920s' there were closures, takeovers, a gauge change and any number of surprises along the way. By comparison, the JER led a comparatively 'safe', and dull, life. The adopted gauge, of 4ft 8½in, remained throughout, and there was none of the boardroom takeovers, seemingly from some 'soap' script. The JER lacked the dramatics and calamities of its neighbour, and also the periodic 'highs'. It was never a wealthy railway, but advanced steadily.

By the 1890s, the JER was running 15 trains daily, each way, between St Helier and Gorey, and in 1896 the beginning of a Gorey–Cateret, France, steamer service led to its happiest years. Through tickets to all stations on the line could be bought in Paris and, to meet with the steamship, the railway was extended from Gorey village to the new pier, giving 6¼ route miles in all. Further advances during the period leading up to World War One included improvements to St Helier's Snow Hill station, the purchase of another engine, making four in total, and a consideration, which went no further, to convert the whole line to electric traction. Certainly that period seems to have been the high point of the JER.

Following the end of World War One, the position of railways began to change dramatically with the arrival of the motor vehicle, in its many forms. The JR purchased a bus company and introduced steam railcars in the early 1920s, these serving it well throughout the decade. The JER, on the other hand, vacillated, did not purchase a bus competitor until 1926, while the first steam railcars did not arrive until the following year. These rearguard actions came too late to save, and perhaps even hastened the demise of, the company. The bus concern was a failure from the outset, and the JER incurred losses each year from 1925 onwards, at the very time when the JR was enjoying its most successful period.

An approach was made in 1928 to the JR concerning a possible merger, but this was, sensibly, rejected; why should a soaring swan want to help a bedraggled, lame duck, especially when storm clouds were approaching on the horizon? The end came in June the following year, when both railway and bus operations were simultaneously closed. This was quite probably the most dramatic, and spontaneous incident in the existence of the JER, which had sauntered along, seemingly unaware of the magnitudinous effect the motor vehicle would have on railways. The old 0-4-2Ts and their little four-wheeled coaches rattled along the rails no more; an early victim of the motor car which now dominates so much of our lives, and virtually paralyses the island.

Jersey Eastern Railway Mont Orgueil, *built by Kitson in 1886, stands at Gorey Pier station, in front of the dramatically situated castle, from which it has taken its name; the end of the line for the railway, and also this collection. This standard gauge 0-4-2T had 13in x 20in cylinders, 140psi boiler pressure, 4ft driving wheels, weighed 25 tons and, as such, was representative of all the JER engines. This was the station built to connect with the steamer service to Cateret, which gave the JER the prestige of through tickets, for all its stations, being available from Paris, and beyond. Further down the train, a wheeltapper, whose familiar 'ring' was such an essential part of the 'magic' of travel by train and whose task is one of the very many that have vanished from the scene, goes about his task.*

Glossary

Certain railway enthusiasts and historians consider a glossary to be an unnecessary inclusion in such a book as this. However, after being infuriated on many occasions, while undertaking the research for this book, and being unable to trace the company set of initials referred to, I feel that such an aid will be of benefit to most readers, at some point.

The company initials, as I have used them, will be followed, if necessary, by the initials of the 'pre Grouping' company it was absorbed by.

Initials	Company	Absorbed by
A(NSW)DR	Alexandra (Newport & South Wales) Docks & Railway	
BGR	Birmingham & Glouceter Railway	MR
BMTJctR	Brecon & Merthyr Tydfil Junction Railway	
BR	British Rail	
CR	Caledonian Railway	
CamR	Cambrian Railways	
CLC	Cheshire Lines Committee	GCR/GNR/MR
DKR	Dublin & Kingstown Railway	DWWR
DSER	Dublin & South Eastern Railway	
DWWR	Dublin, Wicklow & Western Railway	DSER
EWJctR	East & West Junction Railway	SMJctR
ECR	Eastern Counties Railway	GER
ELR	East London Railway	MetR
FoxR	Foxdale Railway	IMR
FR	Furness Railway	
G&SWR	Glasgow & South Western Railway	
GJctR	Grand Junction Railway	LNWR
GCR	Great Central Railway	
GER	Great Eastern Railway	
GNSR	Great North of Scotland Railway	
GNR	Great Northern Railway	
GtSWR	Great Southern & Western Railway (Ireland)	
GWR	Great Western Railway	
HR	Highland Railway	
HBR	Hull & Barnsley Railway	NER
IMR	Isle of Man Railway	
JER	Jersey Eastern Railway	
JR	Jersey Railway	
JRT	Jersey Railways & Tramway Limited	
LYR	Lancashire & Yorkshire Railway	LNWR
LMR	Liverpool & Manchester Railway	LNWR
LBirmR	London & Birmingham Railway	LNWR
LBrR	London & Brighton Railway	LBSCR
LBR	London & Blackwall Railway	GER
LCR	London & Croydon Railway	LBSCR
LNER	London & North Eastern Railway	
LNWR	London & North Western Railway	
LSWR	London & South Western Railway	
LBSCR	London, Brighton & South Coast Railway	
LCDR	London, Chatham & Dover Railway	SECR
LMS	London, Midland & Scottish Railway	
LTSExtR	London, Tilbury & Southend Extension Railway	LTSR
LTSR	London, Tilbury & Southend Railway	MR
L&BR	Lynton & Barnstaple Railway	
MSLR	Manchester, Sheffield & Lincolnshire Railway	GCR
MNR	Manx Northern Railway	IMR
MerR	Mersey Railway	
MDR	Metropolitan District Railway	
MetR	Metropolitan Railway	
MGNJtR	Midland & Great Northern Joint Railway	
MSWJctR	Midland & South Western Junction Railway	
MGWR	Midland Great Western Railway (Ireland)	
MR	Midland Railway	
MER	Millwall Extension Railway	PLA
NBR	North British Railway	
NER	North Eastern Railway	
NLR	North London Railway	LNWR
NSR	North Staffordshire Railway	
NSWJctR	North & South Western Junction Railway	
NBJctR	Northampton & Banbury Junction Railway	SMJctR
PLA	Port of London Authority (Docks)	
PWR	Portpatrick & Wigtownshire Railway	MR/LNWR/GSWR/CR
RR	Rhymney Railway	
SDR	Somerset & Dorset Railway	LSWR/MR
SECR	South Eastern & Chatham Railway	
SER	South Eastern Railway	SECR
SR	Southern Railway	
SMJctR	Stratford on Avon & Midland Junction Railway	
SMAR	Swindon, Marlborough & Andover Railway	MSWJctR
TVR	Taff Vale Railway	
WLWR	Waterford, Limerick & Western Railway	GtSWR
WFJctR	Whitehaven & Furness Junction Railway	FR
WR	Wirral Railway	

in = inches, ft = feet, lbs = pounds, cwt = hundredweight, T.E. = tractive effort, psi = pounds per square inch, H.P. = high pressure, L.P. = low pressure (cylinders)

Index of Illustrations